MURDEROUS M

All SHAPES and SIZES

Kjartan Poskitt

SCHOLASTIC

www.murderousmaths.co.uk

Scholastic Children's Books,
Euston House, 24 Eversholt Street,
London NW1 1DB, UK

A division of Scholastic Ltd
London ~ New York ~ Toronto ~ Sydney ~ Auckland
Mexico City ~ New Delhi ~ Hong Kong

Published by Scholastic Ltd, 2014

Some of the material in this book has previously been published in *Murderous Maths: Guaranteed To Mash Your Mind* (1998), *Murderous Maths: Desperate Measures* (2000), *Murderous Maths: Savage Shapes* (2000), *Murderous Maths: The Fiendish Angletron* (2004), *Murderous Maths: The Perfect Sausage* (2005), *Murderous Maths: Easy Questions, Evil Answers* (2010)

ISBN 978 1407 14722 2

Printed and bound by CPI Group (UK) Ltd, Croydon, CR0 4YY

6 8 10 9 7

CONTENTS

KJARTAN POSKITT's first jobs included playing pianos very loudly, presenting children's tv, inventing puzzles and writing pantomimes. Maths was his best subject at school, because it was the only one that didn't need good spelling and handwriting. As well as 30 maths books, he has written books about space, magic, codes and pants, and he also writes the Agatha Parrot and Borgon the Axeboy books. His favourite number is 12,988,816 because that's how many ways you can put 32 dominoes on a chessboard (although he didn't count them himself). If he wasn't an author he would like to have been a sound effects man. He has two old pinball tables, seven guitars and lots of dangerous old music synthesisers and he plays all of them... badly!

THE SECRET VAULT

SHH! NO ONE'S SUPPOSED TO KNOW ABOUT THIS BUT...

...inside the lifts in the Murderous Maths building there are about 50 buttons. They take you up to all the different floors, but here's a big secret! If you push buttons 7, 35 and 43 all at the same time, the lift takes you *down* to a secret level.

When you step out you'll find yourself in a maximum-security restricted area! The temperature is carefully controlled and the walls are made of soft rubber to stop any draughts or vibrations.

Any stray flies are immediately zapped by laser beams.

When the ancient Greeks first studied maths, their favourite subject was shape. Some of their drawings were done using ink and paper, but a lot of them were just traced out in sand on the ground. Luckily for us, some old maths fans would sneak round at the end of the day and carefully slide a tray under the sand, then carry the drawings home and show their friends. The miracle is that some of these diagrams have managed to survive through wars, earthquakes, winds and rain, and they've ended up in our secret vault!

The shape quiz

Can you recognize different shapes from their descriptions?

This quiz will take you three hours and two minutes. That's because it will take you two minutes to answer all the questions, and then three hours to stop laughing because it's so easy. To make it even easier, here are a couple of useful things to know:

PARALLEL LINES are two or more lines that always have the same distance between them. If you drew them on for ever they would never ever touch. The rails on a straight piece of railway track have to be parallel or the train would fall off.

Parallel lines don't have to be the same length.

A RIGHT ANGLE is a square corner such as the corner of this book. It's easy to make a right angle.

1 Start off with any piece of paper.

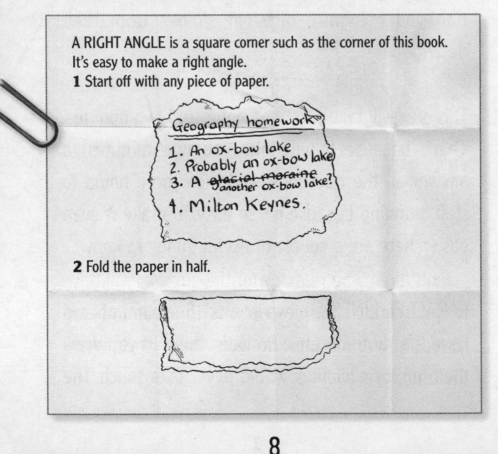

Geography homework

1. An ox-bow lake
2. Probably an ox-bow lake
3. A ~~glacial moraine~~ another ox-bow lake?
4. Milton Keynes.

2 Fold the paper in half.

3 Fold it in half again so that the folded edges meet.

4 Open it out — and you will see four perfect right angles in the middle!

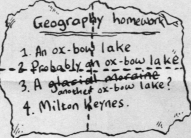

Geography homework

1. An ox-bow lake
~~2. Probably an ox-bow lake~~
3. A ~~glacial moraine~~ another ox-bow lake?
4. Milton Keynes.

When people draw shapes, they usually show right angles by putting a little box in the corner.

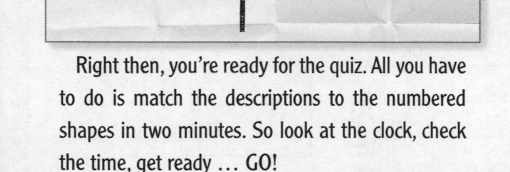

Right then, you're ready for the quiz. All you have to do is match the descriptions to the numbered shapes in two minutes. So look at the clock, check the time, get ready ... GO!

SQUARE

Four sides, all the same length. All four corners are right angles.

SCALENE TRIANGLE

Three sides, all different lengths.

RECTANGLE

Four sides, opposite sides are the same length. All four corners are right angles.

PARALLELOGRAM

Four sides, opposite sides same length and parallel. No right angles (otherwise it would be a rectangle).

CIRCLE

Two sides. Actually they do have two sides: an inside and an outside — ha ha! No, of course it's only one side which bends round and joins on to itself keeping the same distance from the middle all the way round. Gosh, if you can't find the circle shape you're in trouble, aren't you?

IRREGULAR TRAPEZOID
Four sides, all of different lengths. One opposite pair of sides is parallel.

KITE
Four sides, two short sides meet and two long sides meet. Probably no right angles, but there might be one or two. Who cares? The main thing is, does it fly?

EQUILATERAL TRIANGLE
Three sides, all the same length.

RHOMBUS
Four sides all the same length. No right angles. (Otherwise it would be a square!)

THE TERRIBLY LOVELY VERONICA GUMFLOSS
Lots of sides and angles and a temper to take the stripes off a tiger.

ISOSCELES TRIANGLE
Three sides, two have the same length.

ISOSCELES TRAPEZOID
Four sides, two are parallel. The two sloping sides are the same length.

IRREGULAR QUADRILATERAL
Four sides, none parallel. At least one side must be a different length from the others. (The others can all be the same or different.)

RIGHT-ANGLED TRIANGLE
Three sides. One angle must be a right angle.

ANSWERS
1 square, **2** rhombus, **3** rectangle, **4** parallelogram, **5** kite, **6** irregular trapezoid, **7** isosceles trapezoid, **8** scalene triangle, **9** isosceles triangle, **10** equilateral triangle, **11** circle, **12** Veronica, **13** right-angled triangle, **14** irregular quadrilateral.

How did you get on? Did you manage to pick out the *isosceles* triangle? Let's have a better look at it:

"Isosceles" actually means "equal legs" and in an isosceles triangle, the two angles opposite the equal sides always have to be the same size. It doesn't matter if the triangle is a long pointy one or a short flat one.

This diagram is thousands of years old, so isn't it amazing that not one single grain of sand has moved in all that time!

What else have we got down here?

SPANGLED, TANGLED AND DANGLED ANGLES

Whenever two straight lines meet, you get an angle.

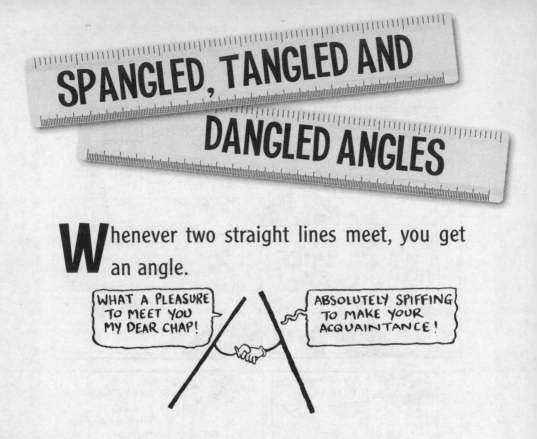

WHAT A PLEASURE TO MEET YOU MY DEAR CHAP!

ABSOLUTELY SPIFFING TO MAKE YOUR ACQUAINTANCE!

Oh for goodness sake! Luckily here's Veronica Gumfloss in her spangled tights all ready to do her ballet exercises, so she can demonstrate some angles for us.

SHIMMER   GLITTER

At the moment her legs are together, so the angle between them is zero. Now while Veronica goes through her poses, we'll watch what her legs do.

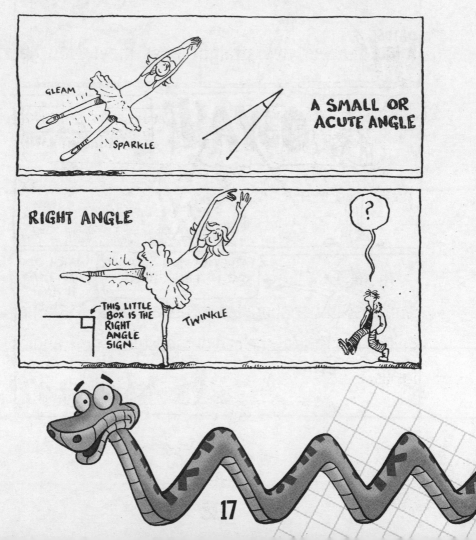

GLEAM

SPARKLE

A SMALL OR ACUTE ANGLE

RIGHT ANGLE

THIS LITTLE BOX IS THE RIGHT ANGLE SIGN.

TWINKLE

?

As Veronica has shown us, angles smaller than right angles are called "acute" and angles bigger than right angles are "obtuse" and you can even get inside-out angles called "reflex" angles.

Angles are usually measured in degrees, which have a little sign like this ° and there are 90° in a right angle. If you put two right angles together, you can see that 180° makes a straight line. If you put four right angles together you get a full circle, which is 360°.

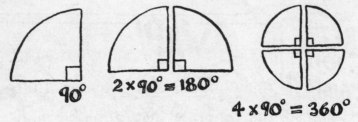

90°   2 × 90° = 180°   4 × 90° = 360°

How to make an angle of one degree

An angle of one degree is really tiny, so here's an experiment to give you an idea of how small it is.

Get a long bit of cotton and loop it round your left little finger, then hold your arm out to the side. Pinch the two loose ends together with your right hand and hold them in front of your face.

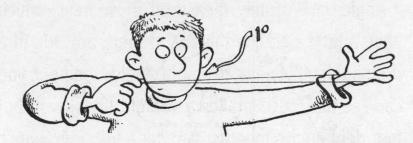

The angle between the two strands will be about 1°. Not a lot is it? Mind you, the next time you're having 359 friends round for the afternoon, you could all make angles of 1° out of cotton and then all get together in the middle and make a complete circle. There again, you'll probably all end up in a knotted heap of tangled angles. What fun.

Common angles and special triangles

Apart from right angles, about the only angles you normally come across are 30°, 45° and 60°. These turn up in special triangles like this:

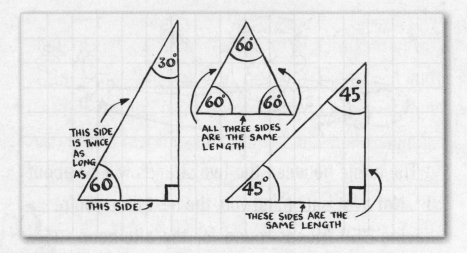

THIS SIDE IS TWICE AS LONG AS THIS SIDE

ALL THREE SIDES ARE THE SAME LENGTH

THESE SIDES ARE THE SAME LENGTH

By the way, if you measure the three angles in ANY triangle and add them up, you always get 180°. There's a neat way of showing this – cut a triangle out of paper, then tear off the corners. Put them together and you get a straight line!

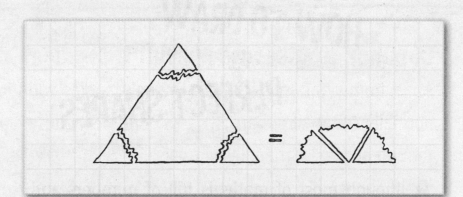

Another trick is to cut any right-angled triangle out of paper. (You can just cut the corner off a normal piece of paper to do this.) Tear off the two smaller angles and you'll find that you can always fit them exactly over the right angle. This shows that in any right-angled triangle, the two smaller angles always add up to 90°.

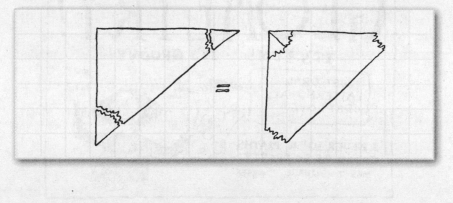

23

HOW TO DRAW PERFECT SHAPES

Although most of maths is full of numbers and sums, there is one very important bit that doesn't use any numbers at all!

Geometry makes a nice change, and it even has a nice nickname. You can call it *geom* for short which sounds like *jom*.

All you need is a pencil, a ruler and a pair of compasses, but some people have a full *geometry set*. It's a collection of strange and slightly dangerous things for doing drawings, and if you've got a geometry set you can try this test out on yourself!

WHAT KIND OF PERSON ARE YOU?

For each item you have, choose the closest description and count up how many points you score. Score 1 for any item you don't have.

RULER (that's the long flat
thing with numbers on
the side)

Perfectly clean	3
"I ❤ Jen Scoggins" (or another name) drawn on it	4
So filthy you can't see the numbers	8
Big bite taken out of the middle	6

PENCIL (that's the stick
thing that makes marks)

Perfectly sharpened	2
Gently nibbled at one end	5
Lightly chewed at both ends	9
Heavily gnashed at three ends	106

RUBBER (that's the rubber thing)

Perfectly clean	liar
Utterly filthy	7

Shaped like little animal *without* head chopped/chewed off	5
Shaped like little animal *with* head chopped/chewed off	10

PROTRACTOR (that's the half circle-shaped thing with numbers on it)

Perfectly clean and smooth	2
Jagged edge like a power saw	7
Two protractors stuck together with chewing gum to make a pretend sandwich	10

SET SQUARE (that's a triangle shaped thing. You might even have two of them. The long skinny one is the 60° degree set square, and the fat one is the 45° set square)

Two perfectly clean and smooth set squares	2
One perfectly clean and smooth set square	5
For every corner broken off add two points	2+2+2...?
If the hole in the middle has fallen off add	20

A PAIR OF COMPASSES (a swivelly thing with a pencil on one leg and a spike on the other)

Perfectly sharp pencil and straight point	liar again
Jammed so it won't open or close	6
Bloodstain	0
Just got one half, the other bit went missing	8
Two spikes and no pencil(Actually that's not compasses, it's a pair of dividers.)	1

MISCELLANEOUS (add points for each item)

Pencil sharpener	3
Half-sucked sweet with fluff	5
Paper clip	3
Guitar plectrum	7
Useless foreign coin	6
Broken elastic band	4
Dead wasp	2

What do you keep your geom set in?

Shiny metal box labelled "Leibniz and Newton Ltd — Bespoke Protractors by Appointment to Royalty"	3
Grotty plastic pencil case	5
Bucket	9

Now it's time to see how you did:

SCORE

0–10   Your nurse shouldn't be letting you anywhere near a geometry set.

11–25   You take maths far too seriously. Be careful or you'll end up being a bank manager.

26–40   Super all-round cool person who'll be in high demand to score for sports events and lead dangerous expeditions through jungles.

41–55   Your brain is a national treasure and the secrets of creation are within your grasp.

56–100 You are an utterly nutty pure mathematician (and therefore your nurse shouldn't be letting you anywhere near a geometry set).

Over 100 URGENT: read *The Secrets of Sums* before proceeding.

WARNING! The pair of compasses have a sharp point, so make sure the paper you're drawing on is resting on something like an old phone book or a bit of thick cardboard so they don't scratch the table. And NEVER take your compasses into the bath or shower. There's no reason to do it, and it could be painful. So don't.

Here are a few simple drawings to get you started.

How to draw a circle

Utterly easy. Just stick the point of the compasses in the paper, open the pencil out a bit and then swizzle it round.

If you just draw a part of a circle, that's called an arc. A lot of circles and arcs need to be exactly the same size, so once you've drawn them, don't open or close up your compasses until you've finished whatever else you're doing.

How to bisect* a line

1 Stick the compass point in at one end of the line and open the compasses so that they reach just over half-way along. Draw an arc to cross the line.
2 Keep your compasses the same distance apart, and stick the point in the other end of the line.

---

*That means *chop exactly in half*.

Draw an arc which crosses the first arc in two places.
3 Use your ruler to draw a line joining up the two places where your arcs cross.

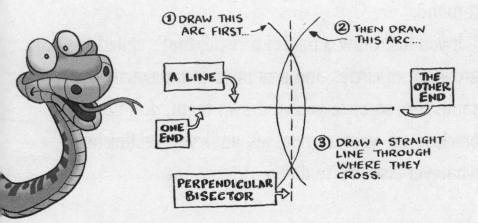

① DRAW THIS ARC FIRST...
② THEN DRAW THIS ARC...
A LINE
THE OTHER END
ONE END
③ DRAW A STRAIGHT LINE THROUGH WHERE THEY CROSS.
PERPENDICULAR BISECTOR

You've just drawn a perpendicular bisector. Woo-hoo!

Perpendicular means that the new line has made a right angle with the old one. When you've drawn it don't rub it out, because you'll need it for the next bit...

How to draw a square the posh way

1 Draw a long line then bisect it. Rub out the arcs and just leave the two lines.

2 Stick your compasses in where the lines cross and draw a circle.

3 Join up the four places where the circle crosses the two lines. You get a perfect square!

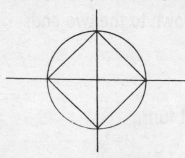

How to draw an equilateral triangle

1 Draw a line, then stick the compass point in one end.

2 Open the compasses to the exact length of the line and draw a big arc upwards

NOW THAT'S WHAT I CALL A BIG ARC!

3 Stick the compasses in the other end of the line and draw another arc crossing the first one.

4 Draw two straight lines from where the arcs cross down to the two ends of the first line.

There, isn't that fun?

And it's a lot more exciting than what the Evil Gollarks from the planet Zog did with their geometry set...

ENABLE THE PROTRACTO-DRIVE!

PUT THE ERASER SHIELD ON STANDBY...

DIVIDERS READY TO FIRE!

WHY YOU CAN TRUST TRIANGLES

Triangles have *three* sides and *three* corners and the most important thing about them is *three* words long:

TRIANGLES DON'T COLLAPSE

To understand this, let's catch up with Pongo McWhiffy who has managed to get the terribly lovely Veronica Gumfloss to join him on a picnic.

SIT DOWN! I'M SURE THE GRASS ISN'T WET!

IT IS! I JUST SAW THOSE COWS WETTING IT!

So being the perfect gentleman, Pongo makes a seat for Veronica. He grabs four branches and ties them together into a nice square shape for her to sit on.

If only Pongo had used a triangle instead!

A three-sided shape will always stay the same, but if a shape has more than three sides it can flop about all over the place. If you look at an electricity pylon, you'll see that all the bits of metal make up hundreds of small shapes. Most of these shapes are triangles, which is what makes the pylon solid enough to stand up. If all the small shapes were squares or rectangles, one decent puff of wind would make the big expensive electricity pylon fold up and plop down to the ground with a big *fizzuppa kazzapp!* (Which would be very very serious so don't laugh.)

When it comes to shapes on paper, any shape with straight sides can be split up into triangles, and that can be useful as we'll see later. In the meantime let's find out all the exciting stuff there is to know about triangles.

The three different sorts of triangle

Here are the main sorts of triangle again:

EQUILATERAL TRIANGLES: all three sides
are the same length and all three angles are
equal. If we were going to worry about
numbers we would say that each angle is
60°, but we weren't so we won't.

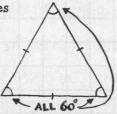

ALL 60°

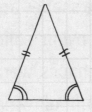

ISOSCELES
TRIANGLES: two sides are the same length,
and the angles opposite to these sides are equal.

SCALENE TRIANGLES: all sides are a
different length and all the angles are different.

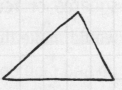

THERE ARE ALSO A FEW OTHER THINGS TO SAY ABOUT
A TRIANGLE:

If the biggest angle is a right angle then it's a
"RIGHT-ANGLED" triangle.

If the biggest angle is bigger than a right angle, then it's an
"OBTUSE" triangle.

If all the angles are smaller than right angles then it's an
"ACUTE" triangle.

SOME OTHER INTERESTING TRIANGLES

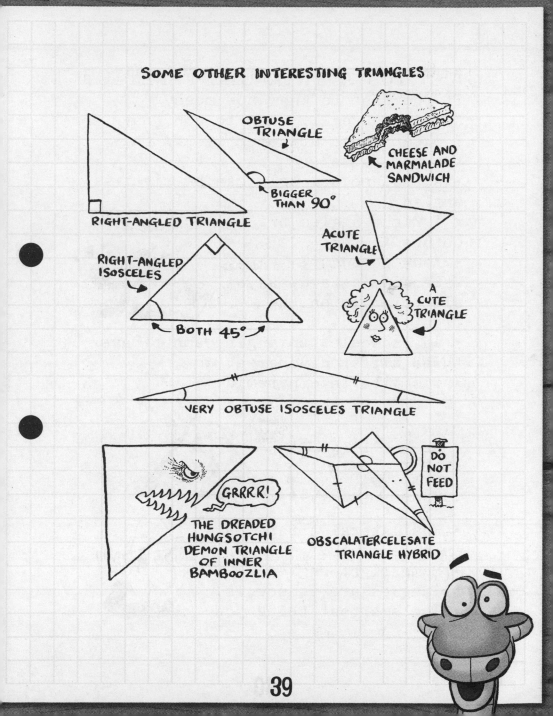

OBTUSE TRIANGLE

BIGGER THAN 90°

CHEESE AND MARMALADE SANDWICH

RIGHT-ANGLED TRIANGLE

RIGHT-ANGLED ISOSCELES

BOTH 45°

ACUTE TRIANGLE

A CUTE TRIANGLE

VERY OBTUSE ISOSCELES TRIANGLE

GRRRR!

THE DREADED HUNGSOTCHI DEMON TRIANGLE OF INNER BAMBOOZLIA

DO NOT FEED

OBSCALATERCELESATE TRIANGLE HYBRID

ARE YOU A TRIANGLE FANATIC?

If you want to know how much triangles really mean to you, have a look at these statements. Are they true or false?

• A scalene triangle can be right-angled.

• A right-angled triangle can not be obtuse.

• Your perfect Valentine's card has a big triangle on the front.

• An isosceles triangle cannot have three different angles.

• You live in a pyramid.

• Equilateral triangles must be acute.

• Some right-angled triangles are isosceles.

• The smartest thing you

40

could ever wear is a hat folded out
of newspaper.
• Sandwiches must be cut diagonally
— and NEVER into squares.

• You cannot draw a triangle on a
flat piece of paper with more than
one right angle.
• A triangle isn't just for maths,
it's for life.

NOW CHECK YOUR ANSWERS

All false: Obviously you don't like triangles. Oh well, it's your loss.

Some true: In the distant darkness of your soul, there flickers a small triangular light. Have hope.

Mostly true: If you said that all the sensible statements were true, and the silly ones were false then well done! You're right and you are also normal.

All true: Take a cold shower. This chapter is going to be TOO EXCITING for you, you weirdo.

One person who would need a cold shower at this point would have been the Hungarian composer FRANZ LISZT because he loved his musical triangle. (You've probably had a bash on one yourself at some point. It's like a shiny metal rod that's bent into a equilateral triangle shape and it goes "ting" when you hit it. It might seem a bit humble compared to things like trombones and guitars, but if you're standing at the back of a big orchestra, adding the odd "ting" in the right place makes all the difference.)

In 1849 Franz wrote his first concerto for piano, but at one point the instructions say that the piano

has to belt up so that everybody can hear the triangle do a solo. For triangle fans, this is the most tuneful and moving piece of music ever written.

Why does a milking stool only have three legs?

...BECAUSE THE COW'S GOT THE UDDER ONE!

Oh ha ha very funny. That was supposed to be a serious question. Now let's mooove on…

One of the odd things about triangles is that you can't twist them. Here's an experiment to explain this:

• Get some pencils or other long straight things.

• Fix the ends of four pencils together to make a four-sided shape such as a rectangle. (Use some tape or Blu-tack).

• Hold two opposite sides of your shape and give it a bit of a twist. Easy enough isn't it? If you lie it down on a flat table top, one corner could be sticking right up in the air.

• Now fix three of your pencils into a triangle.

• Can you twist it? No you can't, the triangle will always be "flat". If you put it on the table, all three corners will touch the surface.

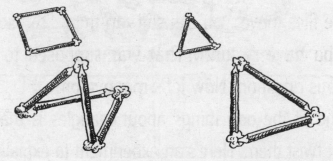

There's a reason for this. The posh way to say it is: "two points define a line" and "three points define a plane". This will make more sense if we pop down to the *Murderous Maths* weapons store.

Suppose you see two tiny flies hovering in the air.

You could borrow a laser beam which fires a very thin beam of light in a straight line. Using the laser you could bore a hole through both flies at the same time, if you point it in exactly the right direction. Even if the flies move, you can still zap them both so long as you move the beam to the right place.

You don't have any choice, there is only one direction you could fire the beam and that depends on the position of the two flies.

To put all this in mathspeak "two points define a line". (By the way it doesn't matter where your two points are – one could be stuck under your fridge and the other on the planet Venus, it's always possible to join them up with one straight line.)

The two flies call up reinforcements and to your horror, a third tiny fly appears.

If you're really lucky, you might find all three flies are in a straight line, but it's not very likely.

However our weapons depot can also issue you with a very long, very wide and very VERY thin sheet of glass. Ha! Now you've got 'em. It doesn't matter where your three flies are, providing you tip the glass to exactly the right angle and fire it through the air from exactly the right position, you can slice all the flies in half at once.

In this case the glass sheet is a "plane" which is a very big flat thing. If you have three points, you can always fit them on the same plane providing it's tilted to the correct angle.

So back to the milking stool.

If you've got a normal four-legged chair, the floor

needs to be completely flat for all four feet to touch the ground. If your cow shed floor is uneven, only three of the legs will be able to touch at once. This means your chair will wobble and you'll fall over

backwards into something brown while still clutching Buttercup's udders.

However, the three-legged milking stool only needs to touch the floor at three points. It doesn't matter how uneven the floor is, you can always put the stool safely anywhere without it rocking. So no rocking, no falling, no smelly laundry and no cow making a strangled screeching cow noise.

THE BITS OF CIRCLES QUIZ AND A BIT OF MIND READING

You might know that the distance all the way round the outside of a circle is called the circumference, but do you know all the other names for bits of a circle? Have a look at this list and see if you can see where each bit fits on the diagrams.

a) diameter b) segment c) central angle d) sector e) arc f) chord g) centre h) radius i) tangent

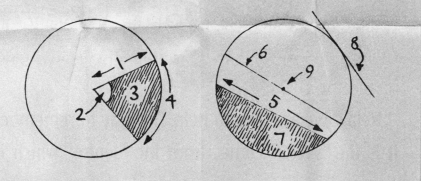

If you got all nine answers correct then give yourself a smug hug. If you only got seven answers correct then this book is going to read your mind...

You got sector and segment the wrong way round, didn't you?

Relax, we are here to help. The way to remember it is the "sector" comes from the "sentor" which is the way "centre" might have been spelt if English wasn't such a wild and crazy language.

You'll notice that the diameter is twice as long as the radius, so it's useful to remember this:

diameter = 2 × radius

By the way, if you have more than one radius, don't fall into this trap...

He's right, it is radii, so when you see this word on page 141 you can feel all clever because you know what it means!

By the way if you have a round lump such as a ball, that's called a sphere, and a round lump like a tin of beans is a cylinder. These both have radii too.

The mystery number π

When the ancient Greeks were studying circles they had a problem.

54

Pi is the Greek name for this little symbol: π. It might not look very exciting but it's one of the most important numbers in the universe!

If you want to work out the circumference of any circle, all you need to do is measure the diameter then multiply by π, like this:

circumference = π × diameter

Unfortunately for the ancients, they couldn't work out what π was!

To start with they used to say that the circumference was three times longer than the diameter, but they knew that was just a bit too short.

The clever Greek, Archimedes, calculated it was about $3\frac{1}{7}$. Although it was very close, he knew that it wasn't exactly right. These days we've got computers to tell us that π = 3·14159265358979323846 … and this long line of mixed up decimals goes on for ever without stopping or repeating. Experts have competitions to see who can remember the most!

HA! I BET I CAN REMEMBER PI TO MORE DECIMAL PLACES THAN YOU!

OH YEAH? YOU AND WHOSE CALCULATOR?

March 14th and July 22nd are π days!

Luckily most of us don't need to remember too much π because 3·14 is close enough for normal people. If your birthday is March 14th, that makes it even easier to remember, because March is the 3rd month, so it's just 3-14!

If your birthday is the 22nd of July then that's also good for remembering π. If you imagine your birthday is a fraction 22/7, that's the same as the $3\frac{1}{7}$ that Archimedes worked out!

A circle trick
- Get your compasses and draw a nice big circle on a piece of paper.
- Put four little crosses *anywhere* round the edge of the circle.
- Join the crosses up to make a cyclic quadrilateral. (That's what we call a four-sided shape which has all its corners on a circle.) Shade in one pair of opposite corners.
- Cut out the quadrilateral and tear off the corners.
- If you put the two shaded corners together they make a straight line – and so do the unshaded corners!

 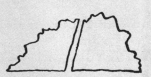

- That's because … *the opposite sides of a cyclic quadrilateral always add up to 180˚.*

SHAPES, LINES AND LUMPS!

There's one question we need to answer before we go any further:

What's the difference between a shape and an area?

A *shape* can be something like a square or a triangle or a circle – in other words the "shape" tells you what an area looks like.

The *area* tells you the size of the shape.

58

This circle shape has quite a big area. The star shape has a much smaller area because it covers a lot less of the page. If you wanted to colour them both in, the star would take a lot less paint.

Now we've got that sorted out, here's a nice little story you...

A fishy problem

In the garden at Fogsworth Manor, the Duchess had a job for Croak, the butler. She wanted some railings along the edge of the pond.

"It's to stop the Colonel sitting on the path and dangling his feet in," said the Duchess. "My little goldfish Twinkle doesn't like it."

"Then we need to measure how long the side is," said Croak getting out his tape.

"It's 12 metres!" said the Duchess.

Croak went to the hardware shop to buy 12 metres of railings.

"Is that all you want?" asked the manager of the shop. "12 metres of railings?"

"Probably not," said Croak, picking up the big, heavy parcel. "But that's all for now."

Back in the garden the railings were in position.

"Perfect!" said the Duchess. "But now Twinkle wants the bottom of the pond covered in nice pink tiles. See to it, Croak."

So Croak returned to the shop.

"How many tiles will we need for the pond?" asked Croak. "It's still 12 metres long."

"That's no good," said the manager. "For tiles, I need to know the length *and* the width."

SCRITCH SCROTCH

"You only needed the length for the railings!" said Croak.

"That's because railings are in a *line*. The tiles cover a big flat *area* and I need two measurements to work out area."

Croak walked all the way back to the manor and got his tape out again.

"Do we really need *two* measurements?" asked the Duchess.

"Apparently so, madam," said Croak.

FIVE METRES WIDE...

Back in the hardware shop…

"The pond is 12 metres long by five metres wide," said Croak.

"That's good," said the manager. "As it's a

rectangle, I just multiply the length by the width to get the area."

So the manager did the sum. 12×5 = 60.

"The bottom of your pond is sixty square metres," said the manager.

"*Square* metres?" puzzled Croak. "What's a square metre?"

"It's a square that measures one metre along each side," said the manager. "One box of tiles covers one square metre, so you'll need sixty boxes."

"What I really need is a lorry to carry them all," moaned Croak.

Eventually the bottom of the pond was tiled.

"Will that be all, madam?" asked Croak.

"Of course not!" said the Duchess. "Twinkle needs some new water."

"I'll get the hose pipe," said Croak.

"Not likely!" said the Duchess. "Twinkle doesn't like common tap water. Go and get some posh pond water."

So Croak went all the way back to the hardware shop.

"Posh pond water?" asked the manager. "How much do you need?"

"The pond is 12 metres long by five metres wide," said Croak.

"I know that!" laughed the manager. "But how deep is it?"

"Deep?" gasped Croak. "You didn't need to know that for the tiles."

"That's because tiles are *area*," said the manager. "Water is *volume*. It takes up a great big lumpy space. I need three measurements to work out volume."

"Oh no!" muttered Croak. "Not another measurement!"

Back at the manor, the Duchess was bewildered.

"So for water, we need to know the length *and* the width *and* the depth?" asked the Duchess.

"It seems so, m'lady," said Croak.

The Duchess tied a stone to the end of the tape, then dangled it down into the pond.

PLOP!

"It's one-and-a-half metres," she said.

By the time Croak got back to the hardware shop, his feet were killing him.

The manager multiplied the length by the width by the depth to get the volume. $12 \times 5 \times 1\frac{1}{2} = 90$.

"It comes to 90 cubic metres," said the manager.

"What's a *cubic* metre?" asked Croak, then immediately wished he hadn't.

"It's like a solid box which is one metre long, one metre wide and one metre high."

"Oh, brilliant," said Croak. "Not only do my feet hurt, now you're making my brain hurt."

"That's nothing," sniggered the manager. "There are 1,000 litres of water in one cubic metre, and it weighs one tonne. You'll need to carry 90 tonnes of water home. Your arms will be hurting too!"

It took Croak many more trips to and from the store before the last bottle was finally tipped into the pond.

The Duchess held up Twinkle's bowl so the goldfish could have a look.

"Look what Mummy's got for her little treasure…" cooed the Duchess. "Isn't it lovely?"

Twinkle yawned and turned away. Croak gave her a murderous look. He guessed what was coming next…

"Doesn't Twinkle like her pond?" asked the Duchess. "Does she prefer her cosy little bowl? That's all right then, Croak can fill it all in and make us a nice summer house instead."

Why do you sometimes need more measurements than others?

Look at this road…

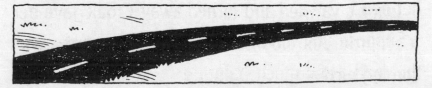

Suppose you run right along it – how far do you go?

Does it depend on:

- how long the road is? (Yes – 300 metres)
- how wide the road is? (No)
- how deep the road's foundations are? (No)

The length of the road is a *line* so the answer only needs one number. This is called a *linear* measurement, e.g. 300 metres. This is like when the Duchess measured for the new fence to go alongside her pond.

Suppose you have to paint the whole surface of the road. How much painting do you need to do?

Does it depend on:

- how long the road is? (Yes – 300 metres)
- how wide the road is? (Yes – 4 metres)
- how deep the road's foundations are? (No)

The surface of the road is a *shape*, so the answer needs *two* numbers (which are then usually multiplied together). This gives an *area* measurement. In this case the area works out to be: 300×4 = 1,200 *square* metres. When the Duchess wanted her pond tiled, this was an area too.

Suppose you have to dig up the whole road. How much digging do you need to do? Does it depend on:

- how long the road is? (Yes – 300 metres)
- how wide the road is? (Yes – 4 metres)
- how deep the road's foundations are? (Yes – so we'd better check)

THE FOUNDATIONS ARE TWO METRES DEEP

The big heavy lump of road is a *solid*, so the answer needs *three* numbers (which are then usually multiplied together). This gives a *volume* measurement. In this case you'd have to dig up 300×4×2 which comes to 2,400 *cubic* metres. We also had to work out a volume when the Duchess wanted to fill her pond with water.

Here are the three things to remember:

• LINE has a linear measurement e.g. metres

• SHAPE has an area measurement e.g. square metres

• SOLID has a volume measurement e.g. cubic metres

Things come in all sorts of different shapes and sizes, and we'll see how to deal with them all later on!

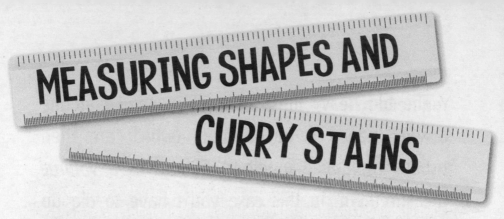

MEASURING SHAPES AND CURRY STAINS

If you're going to cover a shape with something, you'll need to know how big it is. It's like when the Duchess wanted the bottom of her pond covered in tiles.

Let's suppose your bedroom wall is a rectangle and it measures 3 m × 2 m. You decide to paint it bright pink, so how much paint have you got to buy? You need to know the area of the wall, so that will be 3 m × 2 m = 6 m². On paint tins it tells you how much area the paint will cover, so if it says "this tin covers two square metres" then you can work out that you'll need 6÷2 = 3 tins.

The same applies for muck-spreading in fields.

You need to know the area of your field to work out how many tanks of muck you'll need.

Different shapes give you different sums to do, so here's a handy chart to show you how hard the various shapes are. Each shape also has a maths formula next to it. Formulas might sound scary, but they are just a good way of being lazy, as you're about to find out!

FROM SQUARES TO CURRY STAINS

SHAPE	MEASUREMENT DIFFICULTY	TOUGHNESS OF SUMS	FORMULA
SQUARES	EASY, JUST MEASURE ONE SIDE.	UTTERLY WEEDY	a^2
RECTANGLES	EASY, MEASURE LENGTH AND WIDTH.	EAT 'EM FOR BREAKFAST	ab
RIGHT-ANGLED TRIANGLES	EASY, MEASURE TWO SHORTER SIDES.	NO WORRIES	$\frac{1}{2}hb$
OTHER TRIANGLES	ER... NEEDS SOME SKILL.	NOT TOO BAD	$\frac{1}{2}hb$
FANCY SHAPES WITH STRAIGHT EDGES	NEED BREAKING TO BITS.	EASY BUT BORING	MAKE YOUR OWN
CIRCLES	TRICKIER.	UGLY	πr^2
CURRY STAINS	NEED TO USE CUNNING METHODS.	GOOD LUCK- YOU'LL NEED IT.	????

Rectangles and squares

You can see rectangles all over the place, such as the front of this book, football pitches, bank notes, the sides of cornflake packets and so on. We'll pop into Fogsworth Manor and see if we can find a nice easy rectangle to practise on. Aha! That table looks perfect.

Thanks for being understanding. Now let's remind ourselves how to get the area of a rectangle:

The area of a rectangle is the length of a long side times the length of a short side.

That's a lot of words, isn't it? It's a lot easier to use a formula. We just call the length of the long side *a* and the length of the short side *b*. (We could call the sides anything we like such as *Fred* and *Betty* if we wanted, but *a* and *b* is a lot easier.) Here's a plan of the table…

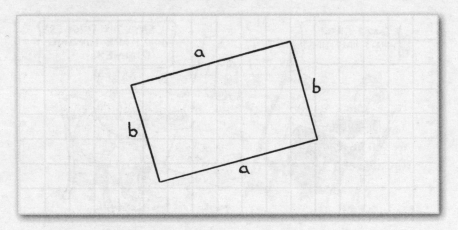

And here's the formula …

The area of a rectangle = a×b.

Now here's the really lazy bit! Because so many formulas use "times", people don't even bother putting the times sign in, they just put the two letters together that need multiplying:

The area of a rectangle = ab

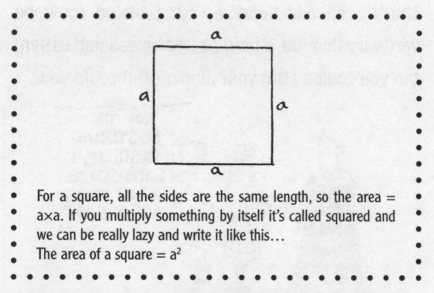

For a square, all the sides are the same length, so the area = a×a. If you multiply something by itself it's called squared and we can be really lazy and write it like this...
The area of a square = a^2

Now we'll measure the table and find that it's 1·5 metres long by 1·2 metres wide. We just swap these numbers for *a* and *b* and get 1·5×1·2 = 1·8. Hang on though, it's 1·8 *whats?*

What do we measure area in?

Remember we measure area in *square metres*! Suppose the area of the table top was 1·8 metres? That's a bit odd because your tabletop could be very very thin like a long pin that measured 1·8 m, but you couldn't eat your dinner off it could you?

HOW THE BLISTERING PANTS AM I SUPPOSED TO EAT MY DINNER OFF A PIN?

Calm down, Colonel. When we got the area we multiplied 1·5 metres by 1·2 metres and this gave us an answer in *square metres* which we can write as m². So we can put that the table top came to 1·8 m².

Right-angled triangles

Once you've understood how to crack squares and rectangles you should find right-angled triangles are simple enough too.

To save writing out any numbers, we'll just call the triangle's height *h*, and the length along the bottom *b*.

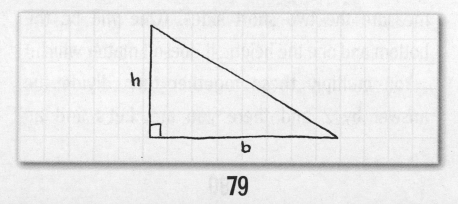

You can see why it's easy to work out the area of a right-angled triangle. If you get two the same and put them together you get a rectangle.

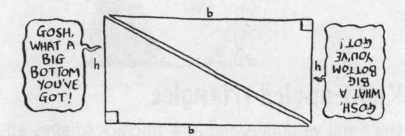

We know the area of the rectangle is the base times the height, so the area of one triangle is half of this. We can put

The area of a triangle $= \frac{1}{2} \times$ base $\times$ height $= \frac{1}{2}$ bh

So all you need to do for right-angled triangles is measure the two short sides. (One will be the bottom and one the height, it doesn't matter which.)

You multiply these together then divide the answer by 2 and there you are. Let's find an example to show you. Aha! That corner-cupboard top looks perfect.

Sorry, Duchess, this will only take a minute.

When we look at the top we find it's a right angle and the short sides measure 3 m and 1·2 m. All we do is work out $\frac{1}{2}\times3\times1\cdot2$.

Calculator tip!
If a multiplying sum has $\frac{1}{2}$ in it, you have two choices.
EITHER: remember that $\frac{1}{2} = 0\cdot5$, so you can put in
$0\cdot5\times3\times1\cdot2 = 1\cdot8$
OR: $\frac{1}{2}$ is the same as dividing by 2, so you can put in
$3\times1\cdot2\div2 = 1\cdot8$.

Gosh! Our answer of 1·8 m² is the same as the tabletop — which goes to show that completely different shapes can have the same area.

Fancy shapes

As long as a shape doesn't have any curved edges you can always split it into rectangles and right-angled triangles, then measure them up and work them out. Let's find one and show you.

Perfect! Excuse us…

All we need to do is divide the nicely polished tabletop up into rectangles and right-angled triangles, so let's get our dividers and scratch some lines across it.

Ahem ... as we *Murderous Maths* people are sensitive types, we can detect an air of hostility here. How would you feel if we marked our lines with cotton held by Blu-tack? In the meantime here's some money so you can go and treat yourselves to a curry at the "Ravenous Rajah". It's the least we can do.

All we do now is measure everything and work out the areas of all the rectangles and triangles, then add them up.

Circles

Exact circles are about the only curved shape that you can find the area of easily with a ruler. You only need to get one measurement which is called the *radius* and then you do a little sum. Let's see if we can find something round to demonstrate.

A round table! Perfect.

It's just not his day, is it?

As we saw on page 49, the radius is the distance from the centre of the circle to the edge. If you know where the middle is then you can measure it. Otherwise you need to measure the diameter, which is all the way across, then divide it by 2.

Now we need this little formula:

Area of circle = πr^2

(Remember π? It's that funny number we saw back on page 52.)

This means that we multiply the radius by itself, then multiply the answer by 3·14.

To see how it all works, let's look at our round table.

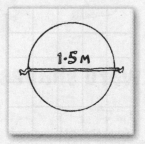

The diameter is 1·5 m, so if we divide that by 2, we get the radius as 0·75 m. We now put these numbers into the formula!

Area of the table $= \pi r^2 = 3.14 \times 0.75 \times 0.75$.

This comes to 1·766 m². If we round this number off a bit we get the amazing result…

Really awkward shapes

This area is a bit more awkward to measure because it doesn't have any nice straight edges and not so much as a hint of a friendly right angle. Panic not!

There's a simple way to deal with this.

The grid method

What you do is make a grid – in other words a pattern of square boxes – over your shape. If your awkward shape is drawn on paper, you can draw grid lines over it. You then count up the squares inside the shape. You'll also have some bits of squares round the edge of the shape, and the rule is to only count them if the shape takes up more than half a square.

Here the squares measured a nice neat 1 cm×1 cm, so each square had an area of 1 *square centimetre* or 1 cm². But what if your squares are a different size? Let's see what's happening in the restaurant.

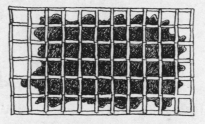

Here we've marked out the curry stain using drinking straws. Each straw is 200 millimetres long (which is the same as 0·2 metres) so the area of each square is 0·2 m×0·2 m = 0·04 m². It might look odd but we can still use it!

Now we count up the squares. There are 31 complete squares and 14 more squares that are more than half full. That gives us a total of 31+14 = 45 squares. We know each square is 0·04 m² so to get the total area we just work out 45×0·04 =…

How strange! They don't seem very impressed.

Oh dear! This could be expensive, so let's run off and hide in the next chapter.

We already saw how to work out the area of a right-angled triangle, but for other triangles we need to have another look at this:

Area of any triangle $= \frac{1}{2} \times$ base $\times$ height $= \frac{1}{2}$ bh

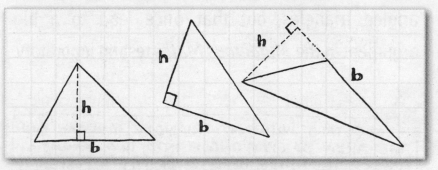

These three triangles all have the same area.

One of them has a right angle, so the base and the height are the two short edges. With the other two triangles you can choose which side you want to be the base, then measure the height to the third corner. Here we've put in some dotted lines to show you that the height is always measured at right angles to the base, even if the triangle has been turned round. You'll notice that with the obtuse triangle, the height measurement is actually *outside* the triangle!

You could also split your triangle into two right-angled triangles, but that once lead to a big argument in the *Murderous Maths* testing laboratory.

IF YOU START WITH ANY TRIANGLE, YOU CAN FIND THE AREA BY SPLITTING IT INTO TWO RIGHT-ANGLED TRIANGLES. HERE I'VE DROPPED A PERPENDICULAR FROM A DOWN TO BC. THE EXCITING BIT IS THAT IF I DROP A PERPENDICULAR FROM C TO AB AND ONE FROM B TO AC, THEY ALL CROSS IN THE SAME PLACE SO THIS MUST BE THE CENTRE!

95

For goodness sake! The only way to calm them down is to get an equilateral triangle and let them all have go on it. This is what they'd finish up with.

Peace at last! The good news is that the laboratory has some nice demonstrations of triangles with equal areas. If you have parallel lines such as the sides of a ladder, this can happen....

I'VE MADE THESE THREE TRIANGLES FROM STRING.

The length of the base is the same in each case, and the height is the same, so they all have the same area.

Ooh look! There are even some interesting triangles in the laboratory window.

The long thin cobweb only has half the base, but it does have twice the height of the other one. It turns out the cobwebs are exactly the same size!

This might all seem a bit silly, but sometimes having equal area triangles can be a matter of life or death…

Benni the waiter stopped singing as the seven stony faces stared at him. He had just come out of the kitchen wheeling the biggest cake ever seen in the state.

"Sing to the man," Luigi his boss had told him. "It's the big guy's birthday, and they're our best customers."

"That's because they're our only customers," Benni had replied. "They scared everybody else away."

"I'm not surprised," admitted Luigi. "It's supposed to be a birthday party, but if we don't lighten the mood, things are gonna get real nasty. So sing, Benni, sing!"

But even though Benni had sung, it looked like things were going to get nasty anyway.

"Hey, Blade," scowled the big man. "Did he call me Porky?"

"He did," replied the man with the blackest hat. "Obviously he doesn't realise that my little brother don't like that name."

"Little?" laughed the others.

"I ain't joking," said Blade. "The next person that says that name is gonna get dangled over the candles. Ain't that right, Porky?"

"Hey, Blade," said One-Finger Jimmy. "You just called Porky Porky. Do we dangle you over the candles?"

"NO!" wailed Porky. "You might drop him and ruin my cake."

The smallest man gave the biggest man a poke in the ribs.

"Hurry up and cut it," said Weasel. "I'm ready for a slice."

"You mean I have to share it?" gasped Porky. "But it's not much more than a muffin!"

"Some muffin," said Chainsaw Charlie. "Last time I saw a cake that size, the top flew open and three cops jumped out of it. It was the sneakiest ambush I ever fell for."

"Oh yeah?" sniggered Weasel. "Pity Porky didn't get to the cake first. He'd have eaten them before they got out."

"That does it!" snapped Porky suddenly whisking a massive knife from his sleeve.

In a blink, all the other men were not there. Although they might laugh at the big man's size, they knew how dangerous he could be with any form of cutlery. One day you might hear the tale of when he took on the entire East Side Gang armed only with a serviette and a teaspoon, but for the meantime we'll stick with the action in Luigi's.

"Where'd they go?" asked Porky, looking round.

Benni pointed under the table, so the big man bent down for a look.

"What are you all doing under there?" asked Porky. "I was just going to cut the cake up between the seven of us."

The other men crawled out from under the table and got back into their seats.

"I'll mark it out nice and fair," said Porky. "See what you think."

The large man very carefully divided the top of the cake into seven long strips.

"There!" he said proudly. "Couldn't be fairer."

"Oh no?" sneered Half-Smile. "So who gets the two end pieces with all the fancy icing?"

"Yeah," said Chainsaw, "and who gets the boring middle bits with hardly any icing at all?"

Back in the kitchen, Luigi was worried. The men only needed to start one small argument, and suddenly his furniture would become sawdust. Luigi was wishing he'd made the cake circular, then it would have been easy to divide it into seven equal pieces with the same amount of icing! All you do is find the middle of the top and then mark out seven pieces with equal angles...

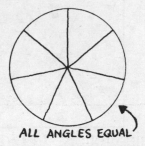

ALL ANGLES EQUAL

But Luigi had made a *square* cake! It seemed impossible to divide it so that each piece would have the same amount of cake *and* the same amount of icing. But luckily for Luigi, *Murderous Maths* has the answer!

On a piece of cake there are two bits of icing. There's the bit on the top and the bit around the sides:

TOP BIT

SIDE BIT

Let's suppose you measure right around the four sides of the cake and divide the total distance round the edge into seven equal parts.

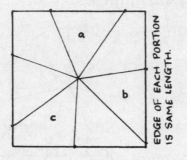

EDGE OF EACH PORTION IS SAME LENGTH.

You then cut from the very centre of the cake out to each mark on the edge. Each piece of icing at the side will be the same length, and so all the side bits of icing will be equal.

The strange thing is that each bit of icing on the top is also equal! This is because of triangles with the same area. Look at the pieces marked *a* and *b*. The "height" of each triangle is the distance from the edge of the cake to the middle. So long as the cake is square, these heights will be the same (remember that you need to make sure your height is measured at a right angle to the base). What's more, we've measured the pieces so that their bases are the same. If these triangles have the same height and the same base, that means they have the same area of icing on top and there's the same amount of sponge underneath. Pieces *a* and *b* are exactly fair!

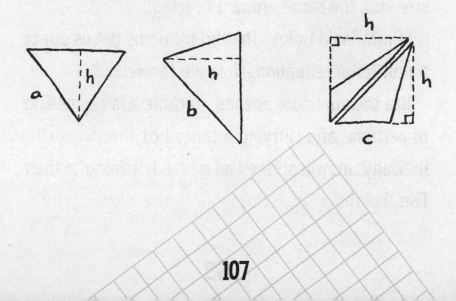

It turns out that piece *c* is also the same size as the others! Although it's a four-sided shape, we can work out its area by dividing it into two thin triangles. Both triangles have the same height as piece *a*, so you can find out the total area of the two triangles by adding their bases together. When you do this, you get the same length of base as piece *a*. Therefore the two bits of piece *c* add up to the same area as piece *a*, and that's why it's the same size. All the other pieces of the cake are exactly the same size with the same amount of icing!

"Phew" said Luigi. "That bit of maths got us out of a murderous situation. Now we can relax."

Just then the door opened. In came a lady smelling of perfume and carrying a fancy box.

"Dolly Snowlips!" they all gasped, leaping to their feet.

"Relax, guys," drawled Dolly. "I just dropped by to wish my cuddlesome chum here many happy returns."

She handed the box to Porky.

"Th-thank you, ma'am," stuttered the big man, blushing bright red.

Dolly stroked his cheek. "Ain't ya gonna open your present?"

Porky fumbled with the ribbon. The box came apart and there it was…

"What *is* it?" whispered Chainsaw as they all gawped at the blackened object inside.

"I baked it specially," said Dolly proudly.

"You? Baking? In a kitchen?" Blade burst with laughter then choked it back as Dolly shot him a glance that would have frozen the toes off a polar bear.

"And why not?" she snapped. "I just bought myself a hot cooking machine thing … what do you call it?"

"Oven," they all said.

"Yeah, whatever," said Dolly. "And this is the first thing I ever made. So what do you think, big boy?"

"It's … like a triangle," said Porky.

"I didn't have a cake tin to cook it in," said Dolly. "So I just borrowed the triangle from a pool table — you know, the one they use to set the balls up. So get those pretty cheeks around it, friend."

The smell of the cake was even stronger than Dolly's perfume. All the others were holding their noses.

"Go on, Porky!" laughed Weasel, "Take a nice big bite."

"And give it a good chew," chortled One-Finger Jimmy.

"Don't forget to lick the plate when you've finished," added Charlie.

They couldn't stop laughing even when Porky produced his knife again.

"I've got a better idea," said Porky. "I'll share it out with my buddies!"

"Why, that's a really kind gesture," smiled Dolly.

The other men all suddenly looked sick.

"I'd hate to get a bigger piece than anyone else," said Half-Smile.

"Me too," said Blade. "You better divide that cake up nice and fair!"

"Oh no!" muttered Luigi who was peering through the kitchen doorway. "Not again!"

Luckily for Luigi, the cake was in the shape of an equilateral triangle. All the sides were the same length and so they were all the same distance from the centre, just like the square. This is important because Porky could divide the cake up in the same way as he did before. All he did was measure around the edge, divide by seven and then cut slices from the middle point.

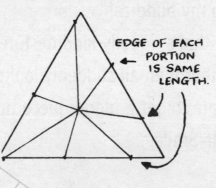

EDGE OF EACH PORTION IS SAME LENGTH.

When you work out the size of the pieces, you get lots of triangles with the same base and height just as with the square cake.

Amazingly enough, this method works for any *regular polygon*. (You'll find out all about polygons in the next chapter.) This is just as well because…

Of course *Murderous Maths* fans don't automatically believe things they read in books, they like to get out there and SEE FOR THEMSELVES.

That's why you're in the kitchen. You've made a plain cake but you need something to use for icing. All you can find is a large jar of fish paste, so you open the top and suddenly...

PISCINE PONG

FISHY WHIFF

WHIFFY FISH PASTE

"Har har!" comes a voice. "Didn't expect me did you?"

Your arch enemy Professor Fiendish leaps out of the jar.

"What were you doing in there?" you ask. His entire body is shining with fishy oil and he's got pink goo oozing out from his shirt.

"I went fishing, but the fish won!" he snarls. "But that's not important right now. Unless you solve my diabolical cake challenge, you'll be taking my place in the jar."

You try not to look worried but he *really* stinks. And even if you like fish paste, you don't want to be shoved headfirst into an entire pot of the stuff, especially as *he's* probably been in there for weeks without a shower. Or a toilet for that matter.

"You have to divide that square cake up into eight absolutely equal pieces," he says.

"Is that it?" you reply. "That's not exactly very diabolical."

"Har har" he snarls. "The diabolical bit is that you are only allowed THREE straight cuts with the knife."

"Still easy," you say. Quickly you chop the cake into quarters, then put the bits on top of each other. One more slice through all four pieces will make eight pieces altogether..."

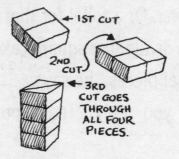

← 1ST CUT

2ND CUT

← 3RD CUT GOES THROUGH ALL FOUR PIECES.

"NO!" he screams. "You've got to make eight equal bits with three cuts and NO MOVING THE CAKE AROUND. Now *that's* diabolical!"

Quick! Before the smell of rancid fishpaste overcomes you, can you solve the Professor's challenge?

ANSWER

Use your first two cuts to slice the cake into quarters. The third cut goes through the cake horizontally, slicing it into a top layer and a bottom layer. This will make eight identical pieces.

3RD SLICE GOES RIGHT ACROSS!

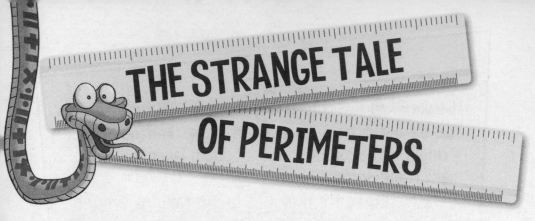

THE STRANGE TALE
OF PERIMETERS

Mr Field owned a lot of land and Mr Fence owned a lot of railings, but they were not friends.

The problem was that Mr Field wanted some railings and Mr Fence wanted some land. As they couldn't agree on a fair deal, they went to ask the judge.

"I suggest," said the judge, "that Mr Fence takes 100 metres of his railings, and sets them out on Mr Field's land. All the land inside the railings will then belong to Mr Fence."

"So what do I get in return?" asked Mr Field.

"When you know how much land Mr Fence has got, you mark out a piece of land of exactly the same area. Mr Fence then has to put railings around it, and all those railings will be yours."

And so the deal was struck.

The following day Mr Fence set up 100 metres of railings on Mr Field's land.

First he tried a rectangular shape.

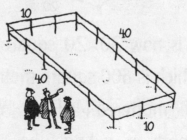

"I used 100 metres of fence," said Mr Fence. "And I made a rectangle 40 metres long by 10 metres wide."

"Therefore the area is 40×10 metres," said the judge. "Which is 400 square metres."

"Hmm," said Mr Fence. "Let me try again."

This time he made a shorter, fatter rectangle 30 metres long by 20 metres wide.

"Your area is now 30×20 square metres," said the judge. "Which is 600 square metres!"

"Good grief!" muttered Mr Field. "You mean with the same length of railings, he can enclose a different sized area?"

"It would seem so," agreed the judge.

"Let me try again," said Mr Fence.

This time he enclosed a perfectly square area measuring 25 metres along each side.

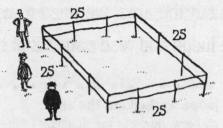

"25 by 25…" muttered the judge, reaching for his calculator, "gives 625 square metres!"

"That's another 25!" moaned Mr Field. "Surely the railings can't hold more?"

But Mr Fence had other ideas.

"I shall arrange my railings in a perfect circle," said Mr Fence.

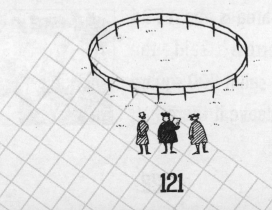

"We know that the circumference of this circle is 100 metres," said the judge. He added solemnly, "And to work out the area, we need to use pi."

(Luckily the judge had read page 52 of this book.)

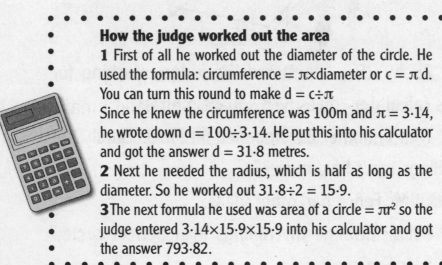

How the judge worked out the area

1 First of all he worked out the diameter of the circle. He used the formula: circumference = $\pi \times$ diameter or c = π d. You can turn this round to make d = c $\div$ π

Since he knew the circumference was 100m and π = 3·14, he wrote down d = 100 $\div$ 3·14. He put this into his calculator and got the answer d = 31·8 metres.

2 Next he needed the radius, which is half as long as the diameter. So he worked out 31·8 $\div$ 2 = 15·9.

3 The next formula he used was area of a circle = πr^2 so the judge entered 3·14 $\times$ 15·9 $\times$ 15·9 into his calculator and got the answer 793·82.

"Your circle area is about 794 square metres!" said the judge. "Let's call it 800 square metres and leave it there."

"Obviously the circle is the biggest piece of land I can have," said Mr Fence. "So that will do for me."

"I should think so too!" exclaimed Mr Field.

"Your turn, Mr Field," said the judge. "Mark out an area of 800 square metres, and Mr Fence must fix railings all around it."

"Just a minute!" said Mr Field as a cunning smile crossed his lips. "Did you say that the land I mark out could be any shape?"

"Any shape," said the judge. "As long as the area is 800 metres."

Mr Field marked out a long rectangle.

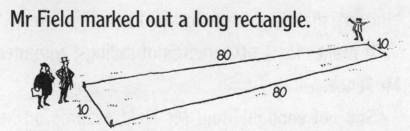

"There!" he said. "Ten metres by 80 metres, which is 800 metres."

"But the railings are 80+80+10+10," said Mr Fence. "It makes 180 metres of railing," said Mr Fence.

But Mr Field was not finished.

"Wait! I want to mark it again!"

Mr Field walked off into the far distance and marked out a very long thin area.

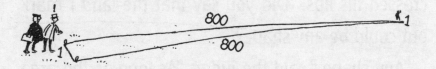

"One metre by 800 metres," said the judge. "Indeed, that does make for 800 square metres!"

"It makes for 1,602 metres of railings!" groaned Mr Fence.

"Still not enough!" said Mr Field, leaping on his horse and riding off over the far horizon.

"Good grief!" said the judge, peering through some incredibly powerful binoculars. "The area is now one millimetre wide by 800,000 metres long – but I am afraid it is still only the 800 metres he is allowed!"

"I shall need 1,600,000 metres of railings!" wailed Mr Fence. "That's 1,600 kilometres or about one thousand miles!"

"Don't forget the two millimetres for the ends," shouted Mr Field. "Now suppose I make it half a millimetre wide and twice as long again…"

The perimeter problem

A perimeter is the line around the edge of an area. In the story, the railings are acting like a perimeter round the field.

You can have several things that have the same area, even though they are completely different shapes.

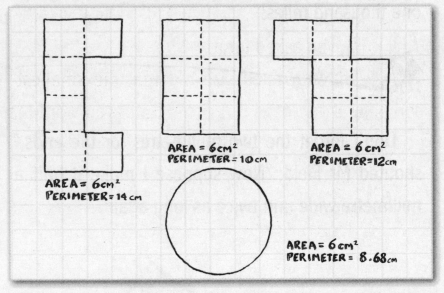

AREA = 6cm²
PERIMETER = 10 cm

AREA = 6cm²
PERIMETER = 12cm

AREA = 6cm²
PERIMETER = 14 cm

AREA = 6cm²
PERIMETER = 8.68cm

These four shapes all have the same area. You can see the top three each use up six squares measuring

1 cm×1 cm, which makes 6 square centimetres or 6 cm². The area of the circle is also exactly 6 cm².

However each of these shapes has a different length of perimeter.

SO WHAT ARE YOU GETTING AT?

All right, you asked for it.

If you have a fixed size of area, the smallest perimeter it can have is a circle. But if you want to be awkward, like Mr Field was in the story, there is no limit to the perimeter if you keep making your area longer and thinner.

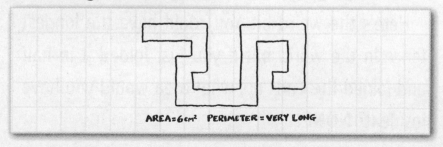

AREA=6cm²   PERIMETER = VERY LONG

This area is also 6 cm² but the perimeter is really long. If the shape was even thinner, the perimeter could be even longer.

On the other hand, if you want to pack as much area as possible into a fixed length of perimeter, then make it a circle like Mr Fence did. If you don't make a circle, then your area will always be smaller.

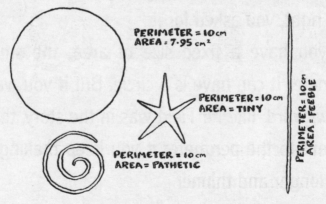

PERIMETER = 10 cm
AREA = 7.95 cm²

PERIMETER = 10 cm
AREA = TINY

PERIMETER = 10 cm
AREA = PATHETIC

PERIMETER = 10 cm
AREA = FEEBLE

Here's the weird bit. You could have the longest fence in the world but if you just folded it in half and joined the ends up, what area would you have inside it? NONE!

Any shape with straight sides is called a polygon.

RUBBISH. IF IT ONLY HAS ONE STRAIGHT SIDE IT'S CALLED A LINE.

HO HO!

Good grief, this book has fallen into the hands of hecklers! All right then, let's try again:

Any shape with straight sides is called a polygon unless it only has one side.

Now you're being silly. You can't have a shape with two straight sides.

Right! That does it. We'll do demonstrations of polygons instead and we'll start with different hexagons. The "hex" bit means the shape has to have six straight sides, and if it's a regular hexagon that means all the sides and angles have to be the same. The other three hexagons are *irregular*. By the way, we've fixed these hexagons onto the page with super-strong glue, so hopefully we won't get any more rude interruptions.

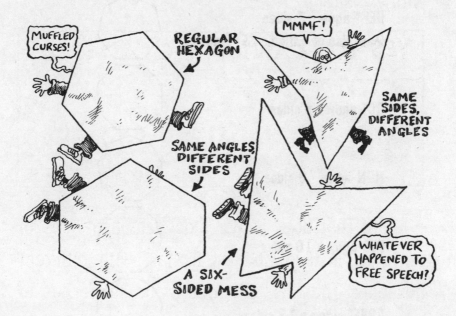

You can always tell how many sides a polygon has by the first bit of the name:

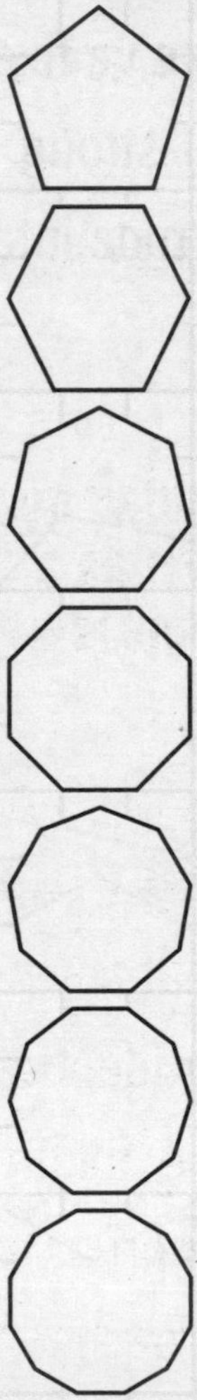

PENT-agon = 5 sides

HEX-agon = 6 sides

HEPT-agon = 7 sides
(can also be called a SEPT-agon)

OCT-agon = 8 sides

NON-agon = 9 sides

DEC-agon = 10 sides

DODEC-agon = 12 sides

These can all be either regular or irregular. Of course there are also...

QUADRILATERAL = 4 sides

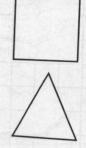

TRIANGLE = 3 sides

A regular quadrilateral is better known as a SQUARE and the regular triangle is an EQUILATERAL triangle.

Chopping polygons into triangles

The sun beat down on the arena as the crowd gazed at the two identical seven-sided polygons lying in the sand. A mighty cheer went up as Urgum the Axeman approached one polygon and Grizelda the Grizly approached the other.

Up in the royal box Princess Laplace held up the golden set square and gave it a sharp tap with her ruler.

TING!

And so the duel commenced.

The princess had been rather clever. Urgum and Grizelda had been having a big argument, which was about to turn very nasty, so the princess had suggested this challenge. The two savages were going to see who could chop their polygon into the *smallest* number of triangles. Although the princess had said that the winner could chop the loser's head off, if it all went to plan then nobody would get hurt.

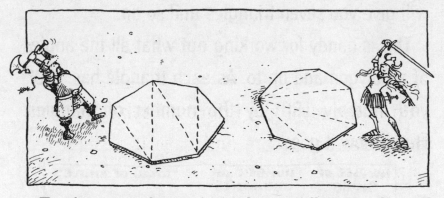

To chop a polygon into the *smallest* number of triangles, always chop it from corner to corner. Here you can see how Urgum and Grizelda planned to chop their polygons, but even though their ways are different, they both make the same number of triangles. The princess had fixed a contest where the only losers would be the circling vultures. Phew!

You can divide any polygon up into triangles, and the smallest number is always two less than the polygon's number of sides. A seven-sided polygon will give you five triangles, a nine-sided polygon will give you seven triangles and so on.

This is handy for working out what all the angles of a polygon add up to. As each triangle has 180°, you multiply 180° by the number of triangles. Here's how it goes:

NUMBER OF SIDES	NUMBER OF TRIANGLES	TOTAL OF ANGLES
4	2	$180 \times 2 = 360°$
5	3	$180 \times 3 = 540°$
6	4	$180 \times 4 = 720°$
7	5	$180 \times 5 = 900°$

RUBBISH! I CAN SHOW THIS DOESN'T WORK!

Oh no! This is such a nice simple idea, surely Professor Fiendish can't ruin it?

HAR HAR! IT'S GOT SIX SIDES, BUT I'VE SPLIT IT INTO TWO TRIANGLES!

Good grief, he's right, even if he does still smell a bit fishy. The trouble is that each shape has four corners, but the angle at one corner is 180°.

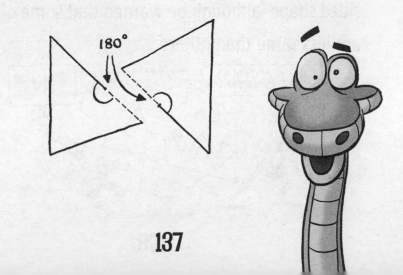

180°

This is confusing stuff, so we'll have to avoid it happening with an extra rule:

You can't make any cuts that are directly in line with an edge.

Now let's see what we get...

That's better! Now you can chop up any straight-sided shape, although be warned that some of them are less tame than others...

IT'S A MYTHICAL POLECTASQUAREXAGON!

RUN FOR IT!

How to draw regular polygons

Get your geometry set out again! We already saw how to draw circles, squares and equilateral triangles on pages 31-34. If you make a good job of them, why not invite along some showbiz celebrities to admire them? They'll turn up for anything if they know they'll get their photo taken.

Now we'll draw polygons with more sides. The best way is to start by drawing a circle to fit your polygon inside. Mark the middle with a tiny cross and then decide what sort of polygon takes your fancy.

HEXAGON

This is the easiest polygon to draw.

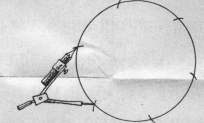

1 Draw your first circle and then, *keeping your compasses open exactly the same distance,* stick them on the edge of the circle. Draw two little arcs that cut the circle.
2 Stick the compasses in where one of the arcs cut the circle and draw another arc further round the circle. Keep going until you've got six arcs marked around the circle.
3 Join up the six arcs.

OTHER REGULAR POLYGONS

Let's draw a seven-sided heptagon.
Draw a circle, then mark the centre with a little cross and draw in one radius (i.e. a line from the centre to the outside).

KERSNICK!
KERSNICK!

GEE, WHAT A LOVELY...
ER... RADIATOR!

We're going to need seven of these radii coming from the middle, with the same angle between each of them. The angle is called a central angle, but how big should it be?

As there are 360° in a full circle, we divide this into 7 equal bits. The sum is 360 ÷ 7 = 51°. (Actually it's 51·428571° but that's impossible to draw unless you have a computerized protractor and piece of paper the size of Australia.)

Grab your protractor and measure an angle of 51° and draw another radius to the edge.

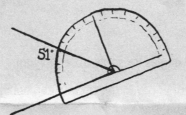

Then draw another, and another and so on.

HINT: when you get to the last line, don't measure the angle. Just put your line exactly in the middle of the gap – so if your angles haven't been absolutely exact, this will help even things out.

Finally join up the seven places where the radii touch the circle, and there's your heptagon!

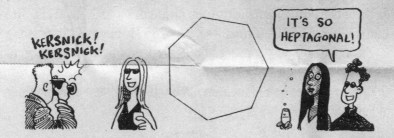

Central angles

Here are the central angles for some other polygons in case you want to draw them.

Triangle: 120°
Square: 90°
Pentagon: 72°
Hexagon: 60°
Heptagon: about 51°
Octagon: 45°
Nonagon: 40°
Decagon: 36°
Googlagon: 0·000000000000000000000000000000000000
0000000000000000000000000000000000000000000000000
0000000000036°

Regular polygon facts

If you've just made up your own heptagon, you might have realized a few things about regular polygons:

• You can always draw a circle that touches all the corners.

KERSNICK
KERSNICK
KERSPLUNK...

• You can always draw a circle that touches the middles of all the sides.

- The external angle is always equal to the central angle.
- The internal angle is equal to 180° minus the central angle.

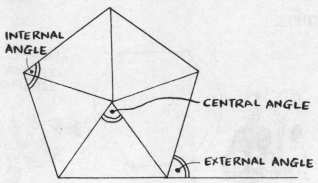

If you want to work out the internal angle of a polygon, first you work out the central angle. If it's a pentagon, you just do $360° ÷ 5 = 72°$. You then work out $180° - 72°$ and find that the internal angle is $108°$.

• You can always make polygons into stars! Just make the edges longer so they join up like this:

And now for the worst thing about polygons...

Isn't that awful? Don't say we didn't warn you.

Shoving shapes together

People nearly always build houses and flats with right-angled corners because they fit together neatly. Of course you could build a street full of regular heptagonal houses, but it would look a bit odd. A block of heptagonal flats would look even odder!

One of the big problems is all the gaps! That's why we usually stick to squares and rectangles when we're building.

If we use right angles everywhere, we also get flat floors and vertical walls. Unfortunately there is one bad thing about this — we're wasting bricks and concrete! We could use exactly the same amount of stuff to build a bigger block of flats, so long as nobody minded living in…

…hexagons! Hexagons all neatly fit together, and they are bigger inside.

Of course we hardly ever build with hexagons, but that's because we're not as clever as BEES. If you make a square big enough to hold 500 bees, then you bend the walls into a hexagon shape, it will hold nearly 600. That why bees make their honeycombs from hexagons! They're not silly.

Strange buildings and alien attacks

One of the most famous buildings in the world gets its name from its peculiar shape. Our *Murderous Maths* spies can now reveal the REAL reason why the headquarters of the American Department of Defense is called the *Pentagon*.

Let's suppose the building was the *Hexagon*. It wouldn't be long before some evil intelligence from outside the Galaxy took advantage...

HEH HEH! OUR BRILLIANT PLAN WILL FOOL THE EARTHLINGS!

BLOB THE BUILDER

149

THE HEXAGON
GOLLARKS AT WORK
NEXT MORNING...
ARF ARF!
CHORTLE
SNORT!
WHICH IS THE REAL HEXAGON?
I'M LATE FOR A MEETING!
I NEED THE TOILET!

The Americans thought something like this could happen. That's why they chose a shape that wouldn't fit together with itself.

BAH!

Incidentally, this information is VERY secret, so shhhh!

Complete cover

When a shape will completely cover a surface without gaps, we say it will *tessellate*. The only regular polygons that do this are triangles, squares and hexagons.

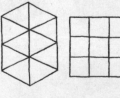

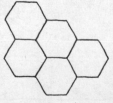

For irregular shapes you can use any triangle or quadrilateral. Otherwise you can experiment making your own shapes with five sides or more.

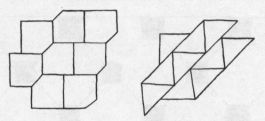

The artist M.E.Esher was brilliant at inventing shapes like this – here's a detail from one of his pictures. Maybe you can invent your own!

Sometimes people use two or more different shapes, such as octagons and squares. You quite often see this pattern in floor tiles.

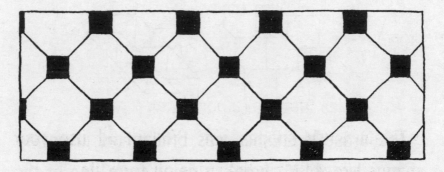

There's just one thing about all these patterns though – they repeat themselves. There's nothing wrong in that, but if you want to try something really weird, you'll need to make some...

Penrose Tiles

These two odd tiles were invented by one of our favourite maths heroes called Roger Penrose.

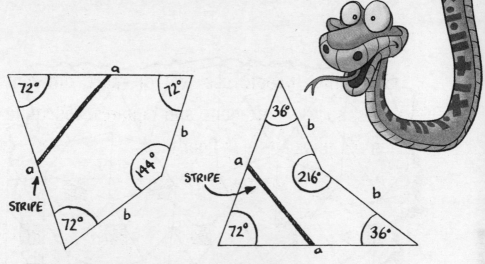

These tiles turn into a good game!

• Draw these shapes out. (You could use your geometry set.) Mark the stripe on each tile.

• Make lots of copies, then cut them out. It's even better if you use different coloured paper. (You can find a sheet of tiles you can print out at www. murderousmaths.co.uk)

Use your tiles to cover a big area without any gaps, but there is a rule:

The stripes must join up.

The amazing thing is that the pattern of tiles *never repeats* even if you cover an entire football pitch!

ALL BENT AND TWISTED

Regular shapes are famous all over the universe. This comes in very handy when you find yourself in the restaurant on the distant planet Janff.

Although it's really posh, there is one thing spoiling it. Sitting opposite you is an Evil Gollark from the planet Zog, and the reason you're here is that you've been sent on a mission to try and stop them invading Earth. The only way you can do this is to show how clever Earthlings are, so no wonder you're desperate not to make a complete 'nana of yourself.

The sniffy waitress glides up to take your order, and you can have absolutely anything you like. You do your best to impress everybody.

Ooops! She'll go back and have a laugh with all her mates in the kitchen. Everybody will think that

Earthlings are just too pathetic to live. You sadly reach for your paper serviette…

Hang on – that's no good! As the whole universe knows, in any posh restaurant a serviette should be a perfect square. Maybe you messed up the food order, but at least you can show them something that they'll understand and respect. You pull out a pencil to draw a square…

The situation is getting nasty. Somehow you MUST show them that a serviette should be square, but what do you do?

The answer is ORIGAMI, which means *paper folding*. There are some nice little tricks to do, and just to impress the aliens, we'll start with this one:

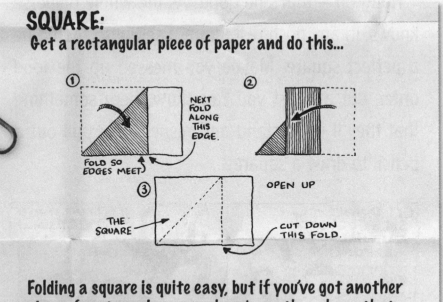

SQUARE:

Get a rectangular piece of paper and do this...

① FOLD SO EDGES MEET

NEXT FOLD ALONG THIS EDGE.

②

③ THE SQUARE

OPEN UP

CUT DOWN THIS FOLD.

Folding a square is quite easy, but if you've got another piece of rectangular paper, here's another shape that hardly anybody knows how to fold!

EQUILATERAL TRIANGLE

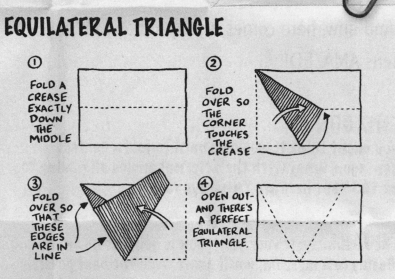

① FOLD A CREASE EXACTLY DOWN THE MIDDLE

② FOLD OVER SO THE CORNER TOUCHES THE CREASE

③ FOLD OVER SO THAT THESE EDGES ARE IN LINE

④ OPEN OUT AND THERE'S A PERFECT EQUILATERAL TRIANGLE.

If you cut out the triangle shape, you can go on to make a...

HEXAGON

① FOLD AND UNFOLD EXACTLY DOWN THE CENTRE IN ALL THREE WAYS.

② FOLD CORNERS IN TO TOUCH CENTRE POINT.

And now, here comes a shape that will leave the aliens AMAZED!

PENTAGON

You might think it would be hard to fold a perfect pentagon, what with the external angles all having to be 108° but here are *two* ways to do it...

The POSH way: If your pentagon is going to go on display in a museum, you'll want to do the best possible version and you need a nice big square to start with.

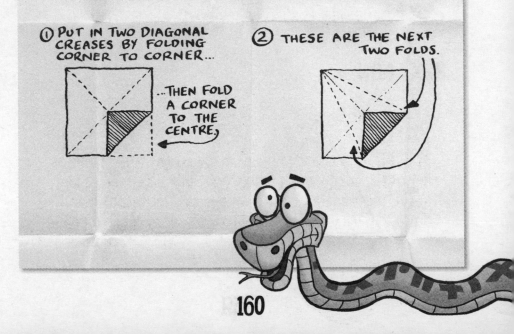

① PUT IN TWO DIAGONAL CREASES BY FOLDING CORNER TO CORNER...

...THEN FOLD A CORNER TO THE CENTRE.

② THESE ARE THE NEXT TWO FOLDS.

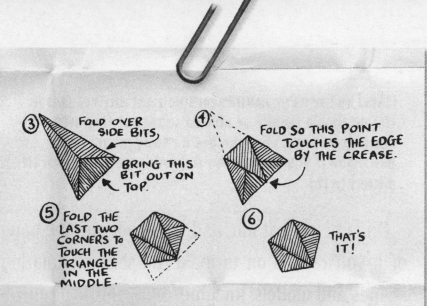

③ FOLD OVER SIDE BITS,

BRING THIS BIT OUT ON TOP.

④ FOLD SO THIS POINT TOUCHES THE EDGE BY THE CREASE.

⑤ FOLD THE LAST TWO CORNERS TO TOUCH THE TRIANGLE IN THE MIDDLE.

⑥ THAT'S IT!

The **FUMBLY** way: Since you first folded a square, things have gone so well for you at the Jannf restaurant that the Gollark even offered to pay the bill. As the long till receipt flies from the machine you grab it and quickly tie it into a knot...

Yes, this does work! It must be one of the oddest things in maths, but to make a pentagon you just need to get a long rectangular strip of paper and tie a knot in it. If you do it very carefully and feed the bit of paper through itself as far as you can before you get any creases in it, you should finally be able to squash it flat into a pentagon shape. (You can get a really smart little pentagon if you flatten out a drinking straw then tie a knot in it.)

Origami is great fun, and when you get the hang of it you can go on to make all sorts of amazing shapes and models. Imagine…

Although lumps and bumps can be any shape or size, five of them are very special. These five belong to a very exclusive club called:

Regular Solids

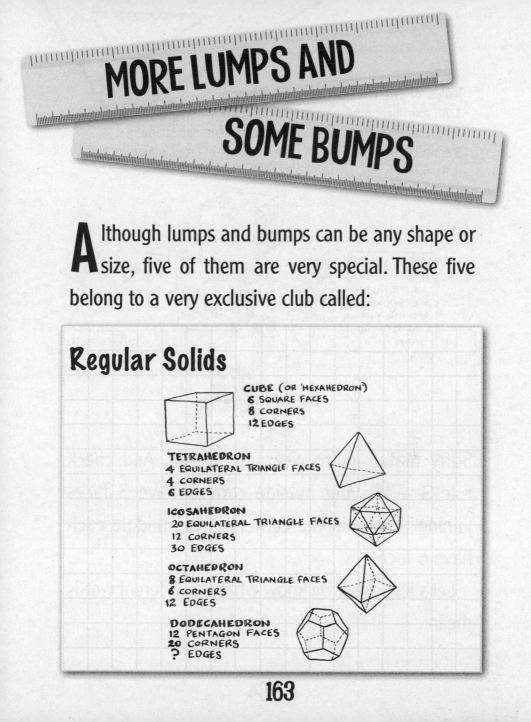

CUBE (OR 'HEXAHEDRON')
6 SQUARE FACES
8 CORNERS
12 EDGES

TETRAHEDRON
4 EQUILATERAL TRIANGLE FACES
4 CORNERS
6 EDGES

ICOSAHEDRON
20 EQUILATERAL TRIANGLE FACES
12 CORNERS
30 EDGES

OCTAHEDRON
8 EQUILATERAL TRIANGLE FACES
6 CORNERS
12 EDGES

DODECAHEDRON
12 PENTAGON FACES
20 CORNERS
? EDGES

Rules of entry to the REGSOL Club:
1 All your faces must be a regular polygon.
2 All your faces must be exactly the same size and shape.
3 Each corner must have the same number of faces joining on to it.
4 No trainers.

CAN I JOIN THE CLUB? ALL MY FACES ARE SQUARES, AND THEY'RE EXACTLY THE SAME...

Sorry mate, you're wearing trainers. And check rule **3** – all your outside corners have 3 faces joining them, but the corners in the middle each have 6 faces.

Let's just check we know what the different words mean:

- Face is what you call a flat side of a solid.
- Vertex is what mathematicians call the corner of a solid. So if a mathsy person slips over and slams his face into the corner of a washing machine, he should tell the doctor "I've just bashed my nose on a vertex." It'll still hurt, but at least he'll look clever.
- Edge is the line where two faces meet. An edge always runs between two "vertices" – or between two corners if you're normal.

Three of the regsols have triangular faces, there's one with square faces and one with pentagons. You can't use any other regular polygon to make a solid that obeys all the rules. If you did try to make an interesting lump by gluing together, for example, a load of octagons, you'd only end up with something looking like an old tissue.

Euler's amazing formula:

Whatever kind of solid you've got, so long as there are no curved edges or faces, you can say: faces+vertices = edges+2. For the cube this works out as 6 faces+8 vertices = 12 edges+2. It always works! Can you work out how many edges the dodecahedron should have? Check your answer by carefully counting on the picture!

The rule even works if you chop lumps off or add some bumps on. Try it out on this:

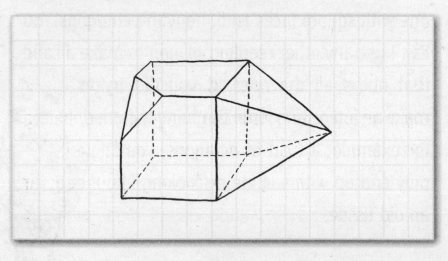

The five regsols mystery!

Thousands of years ago, everybody knew there were only five regular solids, but no one was quite sure *why*. It seemed so magical that everyone expected there would be a link connecting them with something awesome such as the tides of the sea, or music, or the ancient gods or even the whole universe.

Picture the scene: we're in ancient Greece about 2,400 years ago. There's a bloke called Plato who spends his time just thinking about *thinking,* which is a very tough subject indeed. It involves Plato pulling the world apart and putting it back together inside his head, and as the people haven't got football or computers or telly to entertain them, they're dribbling in excitement to hear how he's been getting on.

Plato knows about these five mysterious regular solids, so he's been sitting up all night with his scissors and glue desperately trying to fit them into his big plans for everything.

This idea was such a hit that the five regsols became known as the "Platonic solids". There were little clues to make people think it was true, because pure salt crystals are cubes and perfect diamonds are octahedrons. Everybody must have been a bit disappointed when they finally realised that everything is made of different atoms rather than fire, wind, earth and water. Imagine the fun you'd have if your trousers were made of windy fire. WOOOSH!

A couple of thousand years after Plato, another genius called Johannes Kepler thought of a completely different use for the five regular solids. You'll need to shut your eyes to imagine this.

HANG ON! Don't shut your eyes yet because you haven't read what you're supposed to imagine.

Back in the year 1597, the only planets that people knew about were Mercury, Venus, Earth, Mars, Jupiter and Saturn. Johannes wondered if there was a special reason for it being six planets,

and then realised that they must have *five* spaces
between them.

FIVE SPACES? AND
FIVE REGULAR SOLIDS?
I WONDER ...

Here's how he suggested the planets all moved
around each other.

Imagine the Sun in the very middle.

• Around the Sun is a large sphere with a line
drawn around the circumference. That line represents
the path of Mercury flying around the Sun.

• Fitted around the outside of the Mercury sphere is
an octahedron, then around the outside of the
octohedron is another bigger sphere. This has a line

drawn around the circumference which shows the path of Venus.

• Around the outside of the Venus sphere is an icosahedron, and then around this is an even bigger sphere with a line showing Earth's path. (How's your head doing by the way?)

• Outside Earth's sphere is a dodecahedron, and fitted outside this is an even bigger sphere which is the Mars sphere.

• Next there's a tetrahedron round the Mars sphere and then around that is the even bigger Jupiter sphere.

• Finally there's a cube round the Jupiter sphere and then a sphere for Saturn.

It's probably easiest to imagine how the Saturn and Jupiter spheres are linked to start with. Suppose the Saturn sphere is a plastic football and you chop it in half. You then find the biggest cube shaped box that will fit inside the football. Then you find the biggest ball that will fit inside the box. That ball would be the Jupiter sphere. Got that?

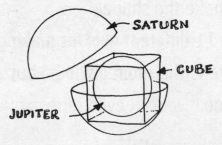

Johannes's idea was completely away with the fairies, which is a bit sad as it would have been really neat if it had worked. However he did go on to have some far better ideas about how planets moved, which you'll see later on in the ellipses chapter.

(It's nice he got it right in the end, because Johannes had a pretty miserable life. He ended up dying in poverty and he also spent ages saving his mother from being burnt as a witch.)

Nets

A net is a drawing of all the faces of a solid that can fold up to make the shape.

There are 11 different nets for making a cube. The big one here is the most obvious, but all the other nets work too.

Here's a little puzzle for you!

The four nets below make a set of dice, but the opposite faces of a die should add up to 7. Can you fold these nets in your head and work out which is the only one that would make a proper die?

HAR HAR! I'VE ADDED AN EXTRA NET THAT DOESN'T MAKE A CUBE AT ALL! I BET YOU CAN'T SPOT IT!

It's fun making your own dice as you'll see if we pay a quick visit to the Last Chance Saloon. Brett Shuffler and Riverboat Lil have spent all night playing Snakes and Ladders, and it all hangs on Lil's next throw…

YOUR TURN LIL, BUT YOU MIGHT AS WELL GIVE IN. YOU'LL HAVE TO THROW A SEVEN OR MORE TO BEAT ME!

DO YOU MIND IF I USE MY LUCKY DIE?

NO, JUST SO LONG AS ITS FAIR AND HAS THE NUMBERS 1-6 ON.

RUMMAGE

As well as the normal six-sided die, you can make perfectly fair dice with four sides, eight sides, twelve sides and even 20 sides using the regular solids.

Here is how the nets look, so you can draw your
own bigger versions and cut them out yourself.

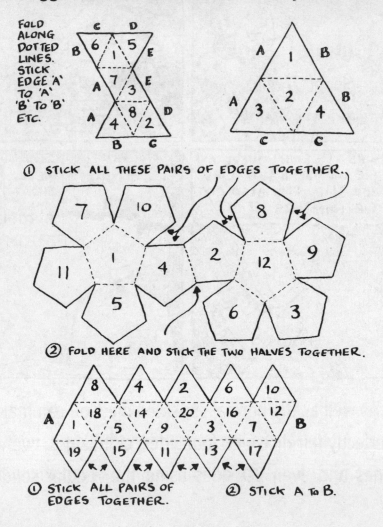

FOLD ALONG DOTTED LINES. STICK EDGE 'A' TO 'A' 'B' TO 'B' ETC.

① STICK ALL THESE PAIRS OF EDGES TOGETHER.

② FOLD HERE AND STICK THE TWO HALVES TOGETHER.

① STICK ALL PAIRS OF EDGES TOGETHER.   ② STICK A TO B.

Moons of Zog

The planet Zog has two unusual moons. Tinjx is a tetrahedron, and here's a complete map of the surface:

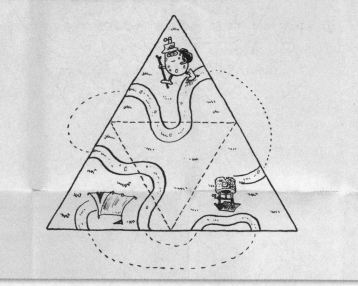

A lonely Gollark is on a camping holiday and has gone for a walk down Tinjx's only path to the well.

If you cut out the map and folded it to make a model of Tinjx, the dotted lines show how the path links up.

As you might imagine, Tinjx doesn't offer much to a relaxing conqueror of the universe, but the octahedral planet Ptuon is more of a challenge.

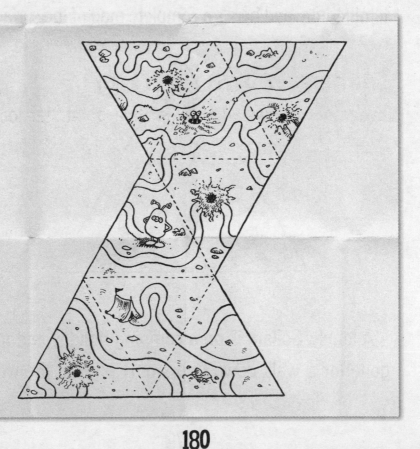

Can you get the Gollark back to his tent without going over any meteor holes! You need to work out which edges of the map link up. If you're stuck then copy it out, cut it out and make your very own model of Ptuon. If you make it big enough you could even go camping on it!

Make your own superstar!

Everybody knows what a flat five-point star looks like, but can you imagine twelve of them all slotted together to make a model?

A couple of the flat stars have been shaded in to show how they link together. If you're one of those really slick people who can draw, cut and stick neatly you can make one of these models for yourself.

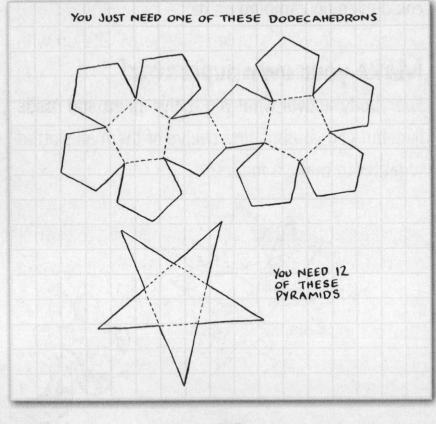

YOU JUST NEED ONE OF THESE DODECAHEDRONS

YOU NEED 12 OF THESE PYRAMIDS

• Make a large copy of these nets – including twelve of the pyramid nets.

• Cut out and make up the dodecahedron and all the pyramids.

• Stick a pyramid on each face of the dodecahedron.

• Get 12 colours and paint each five-pointed star a different colour. (Each pyramid should end up with five different colours on it.)

If you take your time you'll end up having made something truly amazing – and you'll be a superstar yourself!

(Our murderous artist thought it would be dead easy but in the end a team of firemen had to unstick him from his kitchen table. Even then he walked around for weeks without knowing he still had a little pyramid glued to the back of his head.)

Lumpy formulas

We've already seen the formulas that make areas, so here are some different lumps and the formulas you need to work out their volumes.

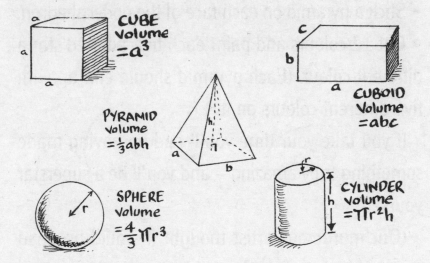

CUBE
Volume
$=a^3$

CUBOID
Volume
$=abc$

PYRAMID
Volume
$=\frac{1}{3}abh$

SPHERE
Volume
$=\frac{4}{3}\pi r^3$

CYLINDER
Volume
$=\pi r^2 h$

We saw the little ^{2} when we looked at areas and it means *squared*. Here we've got a little ^{3} which means *cubed* so $a^3 = a \times a \times a$.

There, wasn't that useful to know?

ELLIPSES, WHISPERS AND WANDERING STARS

People have known about ellipses for thousands of years, but so far there's always been one big unanswered question:

IS AN ELLIPSE JUST A SQUASHED CIRCLE?

Our *Murderous Maths* research team have set up an experiment to find out. Let's see how they're getting on…

And that proves that you can't just squash any old circle and get an ellipse. The real answer is that an ellipse is like a circle with *two* centres:

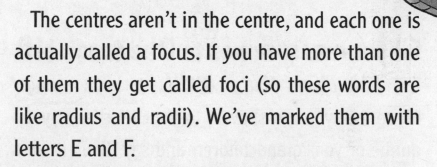

The centres aren't in the centre, and each one is actually called a focus. If you have more than one of them they get called foci (so these words are like radius and radii). We've marked them with letters E and F.

The important bit is that if you pick any place on the ellipse and measure the distances to each focus, the two distances always add up to the same amount. So the lengths of lines EX+FX add up to the same as EY+FY.

IS AN ELLIPSE LIKE AN EGG?

Not really. An egg and an ellipse are both oval shapes but an egg has one end pointier than the other and also you can't dip your little buttered toast soldiers into a boiled ellipse.

Ellipse measurements (the tough bit)

Every *Murderous Maths* book has to have a tough bit so that you can show it to your teacher or your auntie or your grandchildren and say "See? It isn't all rubbish. This book is a valuable learning experience." Even if you don't understand this tough bit, leave it lying open on the next page. Anybody who sees it will think it's your favourite bit and so you must be a genius!

Get ready then, here it comes…

When you draw a circle you only need to know the radius, and that tells you how big it is. For ellipses you need to know how big it is, and also how fat or thin it is. Here's how it works.

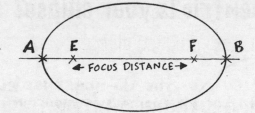

The "how big it is" measurement is the distance between the foci, so you just measure from E to F. That's easy enough but the "fat or thin" measurement is a bit tougher. It's called the *eccentricity* of the ellipse and to work it out you have to measure from A to B. You then make a fraction by dividing EF/AB and this gives you the eccentricity. EF is always shorter than AB so the eccentricity is always less than 1.

Don't worry about the sums. All that matters is this: if the foci are close together, then you nearly get a circle. If the foci are wider apart you get a longer shape.

How eccentric is your ellipse?

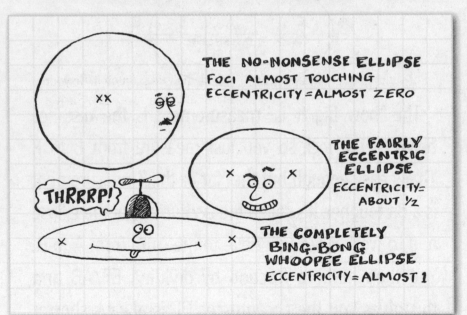

THE NO-NONSENSE ELLIPSE
FOCI ALMOST TOUCHING
ECCENTRICITY = ALMOST ZERO

THE FAIRLY ECCENTRIC ELLIPSE
ECCENTRICITY = ABOUT ½

THRRRP!

THE COMPLETELY BING-BONG WHOOPEE ELLIPSE
ECCENTRICITY = ALMOST 1

How to draw a perfect ellipse

- Chuck away your ruler and reach for a hammer and two nails.
- Ignore your compasses, and grab a length of string
- Move away from the antique polished mother of pearl inlaid Louis XIV desk you usually work at and approach a carved up old workbench.

RIGHT

WRONG

Put your paper on the bench and bang the nails in through it. Tie your string into a loop which goes loosely around the two nails. Stick a pencil in the loop and pull it to the side so the string is tight. Move your pencil around, keeping the string tight. You get an ellipse. Bingo!

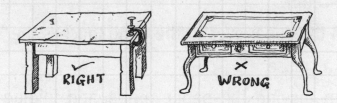

MOVE PENCIL ROUND, KEEPING STRING TIGHT.

The two nails are acting as the foci of the ellipse, and the string makes sure that the total distance from the pencil to the two foci is always the same.

How to fold an ellipse

It's strange – but it works!

• Cut out a big circle of paper.

• Mark a little "X" somewhere in the circle, but NOT at the centre.

• Fold the paper over so the edge touches the "X". Make a crease.

• Keep moving the paper round and folding so different bits of the circle touch the "X".

• Eventually all the creases you put in the paper will surround an ellipse shape.

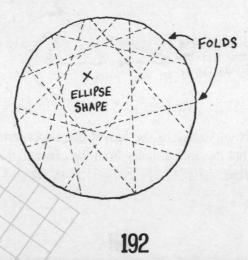

FOLDS

X
ELLIPSE
SHAPE

How to pour an ellipse

This is easy, but a bit useless.

Get a round glass of water and tip it. The surface of the water will become an ellipse shape. (This also works if your glass has straight sloping sides).

Why bother with ellipses?

There are tons of ways that ellipses come up in science, but we've only room to find out about a few of them.

The elliptical room

Suppose you have an ellipse-shaped room with a solid wall going right round the edge. You stand on one focus point and you get Binky Smallbrains to stand on the other. If you throw a ball *in any direction* it will bounce off the curved wall and go straight to Binky. Then if he throws the ball in any direction, it will come back to you.

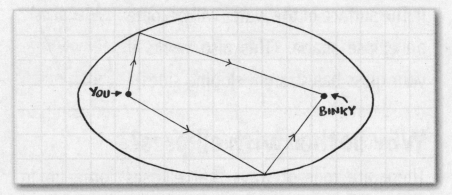

Here's the strange bit – it doesn't matter what shape ellipse you have (fat or thin) and it doesn't matter where you throw the ball.

Be warned! Don't whisper anything rude about Binkie because *every* bit of sound you make will bounce off the wall straight towards him, and he will hear you perfectly. If you don't believe it, then grab yourself a slice of culture by visiting:

The Whispering Gallery

There are several buildings around the world that use the ellipse effect, and probably the most famous is St Paul's Cathedral in London. The inside of the dome is an ellipse shape and there's a walkway that runs right round, passing through the focus points. If you got a big knife and chopped the dome in half it would look a bit like this:

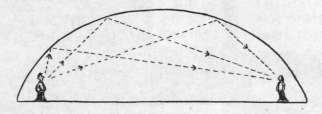

Because sound waves all bounce from one focus to the other, if there's someone whispering on the opposite side, you can hear them clearly even though they are about 30 metres away. That's why it's called the *Whispering Gallery*. Spooky!

PLANETS

So what went wrong?

If the Earth did travel around the sun in a perfect circle, then the Gollarks plan would have worked... but it doesn't! Do you remember we met Johannes Kepler back on page 170? One of his bits of brilliance is that he worked out what shape the Earth really does move in:

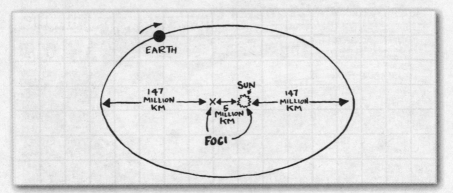

You'll see the Earth travels round a massive ellipse. We've exaggerated the ellipse shape here (in fact the Earth orbit is almost a circle) but the main point is that the sun is *not* in the middle! In fact the Sun is at one focus and, even though there's nothing at the other focus, there is a distance of about 5,000,000 km between the two foci. This means that the distance from the sun to the Earth varies between about 147,000,000 km and 152,000,000 km.

All the other planets travel in elliptical orbits too and remember the shape depends on the "eccentricity". The Earth's eccentricity is 0·017 which is quite small.

• Venus and Neptune's orbits are even more circular than Earth's. Their eccentricities are 0·007 and 0·009. A bit boring really.

• Mercury traces out a much better ellipse shape. Its eccentricity is 0·206 and its distance from the Sun varies from about 46,000,000 km to 70,000,000 km. If you were camping on Mercury you'd find that some days the Sun would look a lot bigger than others!

• The dwarf planet Pluto has the most eccentric orbit at 0·248. Mind you, the Sun is so far away you'd hardly tell the difference if you looked at it. That's why nobody goes camping there.

• Comets are dirty great lumps of ice that turn up, fly round the Sun, then whizz off again for maybe a few hundred years before coming back. Their orbits are also elliptical, but the eccentricity is almost 1 so you get this sort of shape:

Incidentally, when the old Greeks were staring up at the night sky they thought that all the twinkly things were stars. However they did notice that most of the stars stayed in the same patterns, but a few of them seemed to wander about, so they called them "wandering stars". Their word for wanderer was "planetes" and that's how we came to call them planets.

There, wasn't that a great chapter? Not only did you see some top maths, you also got some cathedral architecture, astronomy and ancient Greek all for no extra charge.

What a shame. We've nearly reached the end of our book, but before we go there's one last little job we'd like to do. We're going to get revenge on someone who has given us hundreds of years misery! Remember how we started this book? Well, once again we'll push buttons 7, 35 and 43 and enter the Secret Vault.

Stand by! We're going to open up the coffin and release some *pure evil...*

This is PYTHAGORAS!

The worms haven't eaten too much of him, so we'll give him a minute to recover then get some answers. In the meantime, we'll check his file:

NAME: Pythagoras.
ABODE: Born in the Ancient Greek world nearly 2,600 years ago, and lived in what is now Southern Italy.
JOB: Super brain.
FANS: Thousands of disciples and followers.
HOBBIES: Astronomy, music, numbers.
LIKES: Even numbers, odd numbers, prime numbers, triangle numbers, stars and planets.
DISLIKES: Anything you can't do with numbers. Beans.

WEIRD BELIEF: He thought he was a Trojan soldier in a previous life.

About 2,500 years ago Pythagoras came up with a really murderous bit of maths, which has been giving us some really stinky sums ever since. Here it is:

PYTHAGORAS'S THEOREM

IN A RIGHT-ANGLED TRIANGLE, THE SQUARE ON THE HYPOTENUSE IS EQUAL TO THE SUM OF THE SQUARES ON THE OTHER TWO SIDES.

So what was he talking about?

If you measure the *hypotenuse* (the longest side of a right-angled triangle), then square the result (i.e. multiply it by itself), it should equal the squares of the other two lengths added together.

IT'S PERFECTLY SIMPLE AND IT ALWAYS WORKS. I'LL MEASURE THE SIDES AND SHOW YOU.

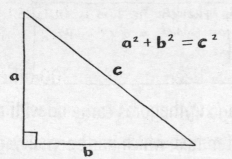

$$a^2 + b^2 = c^2$$

This is where the stinky sums come in!

You see what we mean? (And yes, the sum is right too. If you've read *The Secrets of Sums* you can check it yourself!)

But that's just one right-angled triangle. Pythagoras managed to prove it works for ANY right-angled triangle, and he did it without using any numbers!

Since then there have been more than 300 other proofs using drawings, numbers, letters, circles, tins of paint, cheese and just about anything else you can think of.

Just for fun, here's a really nice proof, and all you have to do is stare at a few pictures!

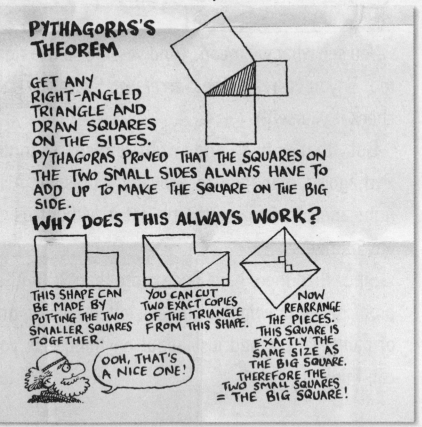

PYTHAGORAS'S THEOREM

GET ANY RIGHT-ANGLED TRIANGLE AND DRAW SQUARES ON THE SIDES.
PYTHAGORAS PROVED THAT THE SQUARES ON THE TWO SMALL SIDES ALWAYS HAVE TO ADD UP TO MAKE THE SQUARE ON THE BIG SIDE.

WHY DOES THIS ALWAYS WORK?

THIS SHAPE CAN BE MADE BY PUTTING THE TWO SMALLER SQUARES TOGETHER.

YOU CAN CUT TWO EXACT COPIES OF THE TRIANGLE FROM THIS SHAPE.

NOW REARRANGE THE PIECES. THIS SQUARE IS EXACTLY THE SAME SIZE AS THE BIG SQUARE. THEREFORE THE TWO SMALL SQUARES = THE BIG SQUARE!

OOH, THAT'S A NICE ONE!

206

As a reward for being so clever, we decided to introduce Pythagoras to all the people who appear in the *Murderous Maths* books!

INDEX